EMPIRICISM AND ETHICS

Moral Philosophers by Edwin Tanner

EMPIRICISM AND ETHICS

BY

D. H. MONRO

Professor of Philosophy at Monash University

CAMBRIDGE
AT THE UNIVERSITY PRESS
1967

Published by the Syndics of the Cambridge University Press
Bentley House, 200 Euston Road, London, N.W. 1
American Branch: 32 East 57th Street, New York, N.Y. 10022

© Cambridge University Press 1967

Library of Congress Catalogue Card Number: 67–12143

Printed in Great Britain
at the University Printing House, Cambridge
(Brooke Crutchley, University Printer)

CONTENTS

ACKNOWLEDGEMENTS

This book was finished during a year's sabbatical leave spent at St John's College, Cambridge, as a Commonwealth Fellow. I am grateful to the Master and Fellows of St John's both for offering me a Fellowship and for their unfailing kindness while I was with them.

I owe a special debt to Mr J. R. Bambrough and to Dr A. C. Ewing, both of whom read this book in manuscript and made many helpful criticisms.

I have incorporated some material from articles of mine published in *Philosophy*, *The Australasian Journal of Philosophy* and *Analysis*. The editors of these journals are thanked for giving their permission.

The reproduction of Edwin Tanner's painting, *Moral Philosophers*, is by courtesy of the artist and the owner, Monash University. I am also very grateful to Mr R. L. Bryant for his technical assistance in making the reproduction possible.

D. H. M.

PART I

THE PROBLEM

CHAPTER I

FACT AND VALUE

The central problems of moral philosophy may be regarded as arising from the gap between questions of fact and questions of value, between 'is-statements' and 'ought-statements'. It will be convenient, then, to approach the problems with which this book is concerned by discussing that gap and its implications. As usual in philosophy, however, this approach at once confronts us with the fact that there are some philosophers who deny that any such gap exists. It will, therefore, also be necessary to consider their case.

We may note, to begin with, that the problems of moral philosophy are not quite the same as the problems of morals. Should *Lady Chatterley's Lover* be banned? Should unhappy married couples get divorced, whether or not they have young children? Should I join the army or go to prison instead? Should I conceal some of my earnings when I fill in my income tax form, if I know that the authorities are not likely to find out about them? Should we go on making nuclear weapons? These are all moral problems. Moral philosophers may not always agree about whether it is their business, as philosophers, to try to answer such questions. A good many of them would be shocked at the very idea. All of them would, however, agree that any systematic attempt to answer such questions will raise some peculiarly difficult problems of method, and that it is with these methodological problems that the moral philosopher is principally concerned. Most philosophers nowadays will add that they are his sole concern.

What are these methodological problems? We may see what they are if we contrast the questions cited above with some others which are plainly not moral ones. Is a young girl who reads *Lady Chatterley's Lover* more likely to have sexual experience outside marriage than if she does not read it?

3

The Problem

Is divorce more common in the towns than in the country?
If I go to prison will I find it hard to get a job afterwards? Can
I be sure that my tax evasion will not be found out? If we
abandon nuclear weapons, will Russia attack us? These are
questions of fact. They may not be easier to answer than the
moral questions, but at least we know how we could set about
getting the answers, even if we have doubts about whether we
would succeed.

Take the easier questions first. The one about divorce could
obviously be settled by getting particulars of all the divorces
granted and noting where the parties lived. Official records
would make it fairly easy to do this for some countries
during some periods: say Australia over the past fifty years.
For some countries and some periods this information would
be unobtainable; so that the question as it stands, in its completely general form, could not be answered with certainty.
But the difficulty is a practical and not a theoretical one: how
to get the necessary information. We know exactly what information would be needed to settle it.

Much the same is true of the other questions. The question
about prison could be answered with complete certainty by
going to prison, waiting till you got out, and then seeing
whether or not you got a job. In the same way we could try the
experiment of abandoning nuclear weapons and then waiting
to see whether Russia did, in fact, attack us or not. The trouble
with these procedures is, of course, that we want to know the
answers to these questions beforehand: we want to be able to
predict what will happen. We can do this fairly accurately by
observing what happens to other prisoners after they have been
released, and asking whether there are any factors in your case
that would be likely to make your experiences different from
theirs. In much the same way you should be able to estimate
your chances of deceiving the taxation authorities. In answering
both these questions we feel justified in making inferences
from similar cases, and making allowances for any relevant
differences there may be between these cases and the one that

we are investigating. The question about Russia is much harder to answer just because there are no sufficiently similar cases to go by; but here again we do follow this procedure as far as we can, by examining the behaviour of Russian statesmen in the past and asking ourselves how closely the situations they were then in resemble the one we are supposing. In general, we base our predictions of future events on our observations of what causes have had what effects in the past. There are, it is true, theoretical difficulties about the concept of cause: we are, however, fairly confident about the kind of data needed to enable us to say that *A* causes *B*.

The question about the effect of *Lady Chatterley's Lover* on young girls is obviously the hardest to answer, but it is, like the others, a causal question, and the difficulty involved is the practical one of getting the necessary information, rather than the theoretical one of procedure. We can hardly perform the experiment of exposing a group of girls to *Lady Chatterley's Lover* and then carefully comparing their subsequent activities with those of a precisely similar control group which has not been exposed to Lawrence; because, apart from the many other difficulties that will occur to the reader, we could never be sure that the two groups were exactly similar in the relevant respects. So many different factors are relevant here that we could never be sure that any differences that did occur were due to the reading of Lawrence's book.

The question is, however, like the others one of fact: whether something did occur, and whether as the result of this something else occurred. Questions of this sort can be settled by observation. In the final analysis we appeal, in answering them, to the evidence of the senses: to what we have observed to be the case in given situations.

Moral questions are not like this. Even if we could know with complete certainty just what the effects of banning a given book would be, there might still be room for argument about whether or not it should be banned. There might be difference of opinion about whether a given consequence (the loss of virginity before marriage, for example) was a bad one or not. Nor is this always due to difference of opinion about the further consequences of consequences. One can well imagine someone maintaining that no consequences, however beneficial, could possibly justify depriving the world of a literary masterpiece, or forcing unhappy couples to stay together against their will, or evading one's responsibility to the State, or allowing oneself to be the instrument by means of which the horrors of modern war are unleashed on the world.

If someone does take one of these stands, it is hard to see by what procedure we could show him to be either right or wrong. There certainly do not seem to be any observations that would settle the question one way or the other, in the way that the sight of the first Russian bombers overhead would settle the question: Will Russia attack us?

Moral questions, then, present philosophers with a problem which is quite different from the problem of knowing what the right answers to them are. It is the problem of knowing what would count as evidence for the rightness of one answer rather than another: the problem of knowing how such questions are to be settled.

It may be objected that this is, after all, quite an unreal problem. We do actually settle moral questions in one way or another every day of our lives. Very often we are quite sure of the rightness of one answer rather than another. We do, in fact, adopt some procedures for answering such questions: why, then, should the philosopher profess puzzlement about what our procedures are? All he needs to do is to examine carefully the way in which we actually argue about morals. We can best consider this objection by examining a typical example of an everyday argument about morals. Consider the following dialogue:

A. Divorce is always wrong, under all circumstances, whether there are children or not.
B. Why?
A. Because a sacred promise has been made, which should on no account be broken.

B. It is certainly wrong to break a promise when that means disappointing or deceiving the person to whom the promise was made, but married couples make their promises to one another. If, then, both parties wish the marriage to be dissolved, there seems no reason why they should not release one another from this promise. It is mere superstition to suppose that any action, whether or not it is the breaking of a promise, is wrong when no harm whatsoever is done to anybody as a result.

Whether this question has been settled or not depends entirely on whether *A* is prepared to accept the general principle that *B* has laid down. *B*'s principle is that no action can be wrong if it causes no one any harm. If *A* accepts this, and if a suitably precise sense can be given to 'harm', the question becomes one of fact. But it may well be that *A* refuses to accept this principle. He may insist that what he calls 'sacred promises' should not be broken on any account and that the consequences for human suffering or happiness do not affect the wrongness of breaking such a promise. In practice, *B* will no doubt say something like 'Surely you don't really believe that?' and will try to make *A* change his mind by citing harrowing examples of human suffering. But this is merely to try to find out if *A* really is prepared to take this stand or not. If he does sincerely believe this, it is hard to say how he could be proved wrong.

A secondary imaginary dialogue may reinforce this point:

X. Slavery is of course wrong today, but it was right in fourth-century Athens.
Y. You mean, don't you, that it was thought right?
X. No. I mean that it was really right then.
Y. How could it possibly be right then and wrong now?
X. Very easily. The circumstances are quite different. Under modern conditions there is no excuse for slavery, but in Greece at that time it would not have been possible for there to be a leisured class without the labour of large numbers of slaves. Without a leisured class it would not have been possible for the Greeks to reach the very high level of culture that they did reach, with the consequent enrichment of western civilization ever since. These results more than justify the institution of slavery.
Y. I don't agree. Human liberty is of far more importance than even the highest possible achievements in literature, art or philosophy.

Here there is no disagreement about the facts. Both *X* and *Y*

7

may agree that without the institution of slavery Greek civilization would not have been possible. The difference of opinion
is whether slavery could ever be justified by these considerations. Here again it is hard to see how this argument could be
settled one way or the other.

The general point is that we settle moral questions by ap-
pealing implicitly to some general principle, such as that no
action is wrong if it does not cause human suffering. If this
principle is granted, then it is possible to decide whether, for
example, divorce by mutual consent is right or not. The
difficulty comes if this implicit assumption is questioned, or
when two conflicting principles are both put forward. The
central problem for moral philosophers is how it is possible to
justify relying on one such principle rather than another. It is
this that distinguishes moral questions from questions of fact,
where the appeal is ultimately to the evidence of the senses.

The point may be put as a logical one. Suppose Y in the dialogue above were to go on to argue: 'Slavery causes human
suffering; therefore it is wrong.' It is clear that this argument is
logically valid only if we assume some such major premise as:
Whatever causes human suffering is wrong. X, on the other
hand, may argue: 'Slavery was necessary in Greece for the promotion of civilization; therefore it was right.' Here again the
argument is only valid if we assume some such major premise
as: Whatever is necessary for the promotion of civilization is
right. In each case the minor premise makes an assertion about
a matter of fact, which may be tested, but the major premise
makes an assertion about what is right. There does not seem to
be any way of testing this except by an appeal to some further
principle about what is right or what ought to be the case.
Moral conclusions cannot be drawn from factual premises
alone: there must always be a major premise which is itself a
moral proposition. How can we know whether these moral
propositions are true or false?

This contrast between questions of fact and questions of right
may be reinforced by considering the different kinds of asser-

tion that may be made about a lie. We may say of a lie that it is cruel, that it is clumsy, that it is unnecessary, that it is wrong. The first three of these are assertions of fact. The cruel lie is one that causes misery to the person to whom it is told; and this is a question of fact which can be verified by observation. A clumsy lie is one that is easily found out, and this again can be verified by observation. To say that a lie is unnecessary is to say that the liar's purposes could have been achieved without telling the lie, and this too can in principle be verified by observation. But what sort of observations would we make, what would we look for, if someone said 'I want you to investigate and find out if the lie was wrong'?

The last question was meant to be a rhetorical one, but one may imagine someone trying to answer it. He might say: Well, there isn't any real difference here at all. If I wanted to find out whether a lie was unnecessary, I would try to find out the liar's purposes and whether he could have achieved them in some other way. Purposes of course cannot be observed directly, but you have agreed that whether a man has certain purposes or not is a question of fact. And certainly we know well enough what sort of behaviour would lead us to say '*X*'s purpose is such and such'. Again, how these purposes could be achieved is a question of fact. We can find out by observing what usually happens when people do this or that. For example, suppose that the liar is a small boy whose purpose is to escape punishment. We say 'He could have told the truth, said he was sorry and relied on pleading to avert punishment'. We judge whether this would have succeeded or not by observing his parents' behaviour on other occasions.

Now, our objector goes on, my test of the wrongness of the lie also involves looking for the purpose of the liar. If his purpose was to save himself trouble, I say that the lie was wrong. Since the small boy lied to save himself from being punished, this action was in fact wrong. But if he had lied, for example, to save his friend from getting into trouble I might say that the lie was not wrong. The test is the selfishness or otherwise of the purpose of the liar, just as the test of the needfulness of the lie is the possibility of achieving that purpose by some other means. Both these are questions of fact.

There is, however, still an important difference between the needfulness of the lie and its wrongness. For, suppose somebody says 'I don't agree that the small boy's lie was necessary even if there was no other way of avoiding punishment'. What would we say? We might say 'Well, in a sense this is true. He could have taken his punishment and not tried to dodge it. It wouldn't have killed him.' But of course the word 'necessary' is elliptical. It means 'necessary for some purpose'. That is why one step in finding out whether the lie was necessary was to find out the purpose of the liar. We were assuming that 'an unnecessary lie' meant 'unnecessary for the liar's purpose', whatever it was. But of course 'unnecessary' might mean something different. It might mean 'unnecessary to preserve life'. If we mean this then the test is certainly whether the punishment would have killed him or not. The question here is simply one of the sense in which the word 'unnecessary' is used.

But suppose our objector says 'I didn't mean that. I am using the word "necessary" to mean "necessary for his purpose". I agree that his purpose is to avoid punishment. I agree that he couldn't have avoided punishment in any other way. I still say that the lie wasn't necessary.'

What could we say in reply to this? Obviously, what the objector is saying does not make sense. To say that the lie is necessary to avoid punishment *means* that punishment cannot be avoided except by lying. If you agree to one of these you must agree to the other, simply because there are not two separate assertions here but just one. The two sentences mean the same.

Now contrast this with 'the lie is wrong'. Here our proposed test was the selfishness or unselfishness of the motive. And we have agreed that that is a question of fact. Now suppose someone says 'I agree about the facts. I agree that his motive was unselfish: to save his friend. But I don't agree that it was not wrong. For I think that it is always wrong to lie, even with a good motive.' Now is this obviously absurd, in the way that 'he can't avoid punishment without lying, but it is not necessary to lie in order to avoid punishment' is absurd? No, it is not. We cannot say that 'wrong' simply *means* 'from a selfish motive', because 'this action was wrong but it was not done from a selfish motive' or 'this action was done from a selfish motive, but it is not wrong' makes sense. We may disagree with either of these assertions, but we can see what they mean. Certainly no contradiction is involved in asserting them.

In practice, of course, when we try to decide whether a given action is wrong or not we do ask ourselves such questions as: Was it done from a selfish motive? Did it result in harm to anybody? But 'wrong' does not *mean* 'acting from a selfish motive' or 'resulting in harm to anybody'. If we use these criteria this is because we accept some such general principle as that all acts done from selfish motives are wrong.

Moral reasoning, then, can get going only if we take as our starting-point some major premise which is itself a moral proposition. The question for moral philosophy is how such major premises can be justified. We know how to justify the empirical assertions that are the starting-point of reasoning about matters of fact. We justify these by reference to observation, the evidence of the senses. Moral propositions cannot be verified by the evidence of the senses. Are we then ever justified in making them? Moreover, what do such assertions mean? If words like 'ought', 'good', 'right' do not refer to anything that can be observed, what do they refer to?

That is the way in which the contrast between questions of fact and questions of value may be said to generate the traditional problems of moral philosophy. But, it may be argued, this whole case rests on a mistaken view about empirical reasoning.

Empirical statements, it has been contended, depend on the evidence of the senses, and any apparent disparity between that evidence and the conclusion drawn from it may be removed by

definition. In other words, the meaning of an empirical assertion is always something that can be observed: all empirical
assertions can always be reduced, without remainder, to some
observation-statement, or set of observation-statements. But is
not this a crude verificationist view of meaning, no longer
accepted by most philosophers? And does not the whole case
for the existence of a gap between is-statements and ought-
statements depend on this exploded theory?

The gap between moral conclusions and the evidence on
which we base them is, it is contended, no greater than (and,
indeed, not significantly different from) the gap between empirical assertions themselves and the evidence on which they
are based. Indeed, there is more than one such gap, and all of
them have caused long, and relatively fruitless, philosophical
wrangles. There is, to begin with, the gap between 'sense-data
statements' and 'physical object statements'. Phenomenalists
have tried valiantly to bridge this gap by the device of definition, and, notoriously, they have failed. Definition has also
failed to bridge the gap between '*A* causes *B*' and '*A* invariably
precedes *B*'. Again, there is the yawning chasm referred to
by those who talk of 'the problem of induction'. Yet, without physical object statements, causal inference and inductive
inference generally, empirical reasoning would not be possible
at all.

It is a mistake, then, to suppose that the existence of an
alleged gap between evidence and conclusion is a problem
peculiar to moral reasoning. No doubt 'your action caused
avoidable suffering' is not precisely equivalent to 'your action
was wrong'; but then '*A* invariably precedes *B*' is not precisely
equivalent to '*A* causes *B*'; and 'there is a table here' is not
precisely equivalent to 'I see a table-shape, etc., etc.', and 'all
observed tigers are striped' is not precisely equivalent to 'all
tigers are striped'. There is no reason, then, to suppose that
moral statements are in some way more mysterious than empirical statements. It may be that neither are mysterious. We do
feel confident that tigers are striped, that there are physical

objects and that we know the causes of some phenomena, and we are right to feel this confidence. We need not lament that we can never prove these assertions, since we have all the proof that is necessary. Instead of lamenting vainly that we do not have what we do not need, we should examine carefully the way in which we do actually reason. In exactly the same way we should examine the logic of actual moral reasoning, and not try to assimilate it to demonstrative reasoning, in which the conclusion does not go beyond the premises; for such reasoning is obviously of very limited use, in either moral or empirical investigation. Or it may be that both moral and empirical assertions are mysterious, and that we are right to worry about phenomenalism, or the problem of induction, or the validation of our moral beliefs. But let us not draw a facile and misleading contrast between questions of fact and questions of value, because there is no such contrast.

But, it may perhaps be replied, we do not in real life come across counter-inductionists, who seriously suppose that uniform laws do not hold in nature, or men who seriously doubt the existence of the furniture in the unoccupied room next door. These are metaphysical disputes, whereas the disputes that arise over moral questions are not merely meta-ethical. The utilitarian, who believes that happiness is the sole good, and makes this his major moral premise, will behave very differently from the Nietzschean who believes that suffering is much less important than the cultivation of a heroic soul.

To this it will be retorted that even such disputes as this do turn out, on closer examination, to be meta-ethical. Moral philosophers, indeed, commonly take as their data the ordinary moral judgements of the ordinary man. Utilitarians and deontologists, for example, dispute only about how these judgements are to be described and analysed: whether, say, the obligation to keep promises, which both of them acknowledge, is or is not derivable from the more general obligation to promote happiness. This is exactly like the dispute between the realist and the phenomenalist, whether our ordinary judgements about physical objects can or cannot be analysed as referring to sense data, from which physical objects are derived as logical constructions.

The Nietzschean may seem to be in a different category; but even he, it is argued, is merely stating, no doubt in an exaggerated and paradoxical form, moral convictions which others share with him. For most men agree that too great a concern for mere safety may lead to a neglect of such virtues as courage. It is not true, then, that the Nietzschean and the utilitarian adopt quite different moral axioms. They put the emphasis on different virtues; but if we examine not only their more flamboyant utterances but also the specific moral judgements they make in actual situations, the conduct they praise and the conduct they condemn, we are likely to find that the difference is chiefly one of emphasis.

That there are, of course, genuine moral disagreements need not be denied: but there are also genuine disagreements about matters of fact. If moralists argue about whether heroism is more important than compassion, historians argue about whether great men have more influence on the course of events than impersonal social forces. It is hard to see that the second question is any easier to settle than the first; yet we need not draw the conclusion that every historian makes his own assumptions about the causes of historical events, and that no fruitful discussion is possible between historians who happen to make different assumptions.

In practice, our opponent may go on, there are three main reasons for moral disagreement, or apparent moral disagreement. First, the disagreement will often be about the relevant facts, in which case, of course, there is no real moral disagreement at all. Consider, from this point of view, the imaginary dialogue about slavery in Athens. Is it true, after all, that there is no disagreement about the facts? There is agreement, certainly, that the institution of slavery made Athenian civilization possible, but may there not be disagreement about the amount of suffering involved in slavery? It is a little facile to say, as was said above about the other dialogue, that 'trying to make *A* change his mind by citing harrowing examples of human suffering' is 'merely to try to find out if *A* really is prepared to take this stand or not'. It is possible to know a fact, in a sense, without grasping all its implications. If, as the result perhaps of first-hand experience, you have a more vivid understanding of some state of affairs, you may be said, if not to know facts you did not know before, at least to know more about those facts. And if, as a result of this new knowledge, you change your mind about the relative desirability of this state of affairs, it is doubtful whether you have changed your basic moral judgement. Perhaps you always believed that situations of type *X* had such and such a degree of undesirability. The difference is that you now realize, as you did not before, that this situation is of type *X*. When this has been taken account of, it may be that many more apparent moral disagreements depend on disagreement about the facts than may appear at first sight.

Sometimes, of course, it may be, not that there is disagreement about the same facts, but that the facts are actually different. For centuries it has been customary to cite, in order to demonstrate the diversity of moral beliefs, those cultures in which it is thought right to kill off the aged. So long as the difference is presented as a clash between two categorical imperatives ('it is right to kill old people', 'it is wrong to kill old people') it may appear irreconcilable. It is arguable, however, that each of these derives from a more fundamental moral belief: perhaps, 'life should no longer continue once it has become burdensome both to its possessor and to his companions'. Apply this principle to a community in which conditions are primitive, life is hard, the old need more comfort than it is possible to give them, and the young cannot be spared to look after them from the ceaseless task of finding food, and one might well conclude that it would be better for all concerned if the old should think it their duty to die. Apply it to a community in which it is possible to provide, not too inadequately, for the needs of the aged, and a different conclusion follows. This is not to say that everyone will agree that it is right to kill off the old, in primitive conditions, but only that we need not suppose that a community in which killing them off is an accepted practice is one whose basic moral assumptions are utterly different from our own, and quite incomprehensible to us.

Where moral disagreement does persist, without there being either any difference in the facts or difference of opinion about them, the case often turns out to be a border-line one. If one man decides to tell a lie rather than hurt someone's feelings, say, and another decides that his duty to tell the truth comes first, they cannot be said to differ in their basic moral beliefs. Each no doubt recognizes that there is a choice of evils here: each could conceivably have decided the other way.

It is true that not everyone would regard this as a border-line case, in which the considerations for and against each alternative are fairly evenly balanced. Some may be quite sure that consideration for others' feelings far outweighs the obligation to be truthful; others may be equally convinced of the contrary. Even here, however, it cannot be said that each man starts from a completely different set of moral axioms. Each acknowledges the same moral obligations: the disagreement is only about their relative importance.

Summarizing, then, the chief arguments against the view that there is a fundamental difference between questions of value and questions of fact are these: (1) Empirical assertions are supported by observation-statements, but are not precisely equivalent to them. The assumptions embodied in the principles of induction, or the principle of sufficient reason, are no more demonstrable than the assumptions evident in moral reasoning. (2) There is as much general agreement about what counts as evidence for moral conclusions as for empirical ones. Disagreement about moral questions is no greater than disagreement about questions of fact, and may indeed often be traced to disagreement about the relevant facts. Where this is not the case, and there is genuine moral disagreement, it is still not of a kind to suggest that those who disagree do so because they proceed from fundamentally different moral assumptions.

This is a formidable case. Can it be met?

It may indeed be conceded that moral axioms are not completely arbitrary, to be chosen by every moral agent just as his fancy dictates. There are at least three ways in which value judgements may be said to be forced on an individual, quite independently of his desires, just as judgements of fact are. First, there are instrumental values, the judgement that something is good as a means. Even when men differ radically in the ends they pursue, they may very well find that some means are common to these diverse ends. For example, they will almost certainly need to be accurately informed about any relevant facts. Consequently, they will, as a rule, value honesty and veracity, in others if not in themselves. Considerations of this sort make it inevitable that men should hold a great many values in common. The judgement 'If I am to attain my end, I need to know the truth' is not itself, of course, a value judgement but a factual one. So is 'It will help me to attain my ends if I encourage others to tell the truth'. The only value judgements involved would seem to be 'Whatever helps me to attain my ends is, to that extent, good' and 'It is good to attain my ends'. There may indeed be disagreement about these if 'ends' is taken as equivalent to 'desires'. Our desires, it may be said, are often bad. But presumably someone who believed that would not make the gratification of desire his end. 'It is good to attain my ends', in fact, turns out to mean 'It is good to attain whatever is good'; and this is safely analytic.

Agreement, then, about such social requirements as truth-telling is compatible with moral diversity: it may result merely from a common recognition of empirical truths about means and ends. It is in the choice of ends that moral diversity is usually said to occur.

Here, however, we encounter a second restriction on that diversity. Men will have some desires in common simply because they are men: for food, comfort, the preservation of life. It need not follow, however, that they will necessarily think these things good. They, or some of them, may decide that these fleshly desires are bad, and ought not to be gratified. That celibacy has often been regarded as a peculiarly good state is striking evidence that a common human nature does not necessarily generate common moral beliefs. Nevertheless, the existence of common needs does explain why there is a good deal of agreement in the choice of ends.

Moreover, even when the choice of ends is not biologically determined, it may be socially influenced. Men as a rule imbibe the values of their society, if not with their mothers' milk, at least with the ice creams and tapioca puddings of their childhood.

All this explains why, in practice, there is a good deal of agreement in fundamental moral beliefs, not only within cultures, but even between them. The question at issue, however, is not whether there is, in fact, greater disagreement about values than about facts. It is whether there is the same general agreement about how moral questions should be settled as there is about questions of fact.

Nothing that has been said need lead us to deny that empirical assertions do have one very close connection with observation-statements that moral assertions do not seem to have. In the very simplest cases, an empirical assertion may be a mere record of what is observed. The controversy between realists and phenomenalists need not make us doubt this, since it is common ground that my seeing a table, your seeing a table, etc., does entitle us to say that a table is there, though there may be disagreement about whether a table is to be regarded as a bundle of sense data or an independently existing external object. No moral statement has this direct relation to what may be observed.

There are, however, other kinds of empirical statement which are not merely records of the evidence on which they are based. One example would be causal statements. Another

would be counter-factual conditionals. To take an example of
A. C. Ewing's: Just as the state of affairs in which the cat is on
the mat makes the statement 'the cat is on the mat' true, so
'the nature of sky-scrapers is such as to imply the truth of the
proposition that, if I had jumped from the top floor of the
Woolworth Building in New York and my fall had not been
broken, I should have been killed'.[1] The failure to recognize
that there are different kinds of empirical assertion, related in
different ways to the facts which make them true, has led some
philosophers to suppose that there must be some kind of
'subsistent' fact to which counter-factual conditionals correspond. But, Ewing argues, there is no need to suppose this,
for correspondence is not the only relation which holds between a given state of affairs and the statements it makes true.
And, if we are prepared to grant this, we may also grant that
(for example) the state of affairs in which an action is intended
to cause pain wantonly makes it true that that action is wrong,
though the statement 'the action is wrong' is not merely a
record or description of that state of affairs. In each case admittedly it is not easy to pin down the precise relation that
exists between the state of affairs and the statement it makes
true. Even the simplest of these relations, correspondence, has
caused philosophers much trouble. The relation between
counter-factual conditionals and their grounds, or between
moral assertions and their grounds, is doubtless even more
obscure. But it need not be supposed that the problem is
peculiar to moral assertions.

There are, however, two separate questions here, which
should not be confused. With a straightforward descriptive statement the referent is also the evidence for it. There are, however,
two separate questions that may be asked about counter-factual
conditionals. One is: What evidence supports the assertion
that, if Ewing had jumped from the Woolworth Building,
he would have been killed? (What facts 'make it true'?) The

[1] *Second Thoughts in Moral Philosophy* (London: Routledge and Kegan Paul, 1959),
p. 45.

other is: How is a counter-factual conditional, which by hypothesis refers to something that could not be observed, since it did not happen, related to the kind of thing that could be observed? What is the relation between: 'If Ewing had jumped he would have been killed', and such observation-statements as 'Ewing jumped and was killed'?

In precisely the same way, there are two separate problems about moral statements. The ground on which we say that X is wrong commonly is some such statement as 'X is intended to cause suffering'. There is certainly a problem about the validity of this inference. But there is another, different, problem as well: What are the referents of such terms as 'wrong'? What precisely is being said? That (for example) X has the quality (which is perhaps a very special kind of quality) of wrongness, or that the speaker has a special kind of attitude to X?

While the distinction between questions of value and questions of fact is usually regarded as a way of drawing attention to both these problems, at the moment it is the question about evidence which concerns us. And the question is not whether any doubts may be raised about the validity of the inference which, it is agreed, we all do make from observed facts to counter-factual conditionals on the one hand, or to moral assertions on the other. It is whether we are in fact equally agreed, in each case, about what that evidence is.

Counter-factual conditionals like 'If Ewing had jumped, he would have been killed' are based on causal statements. We venture such assertions because we know that falling from a sufficiently great height on to something hard is a cause of death. Now, whatever philosophical problems there may be about causation, it is not really the case that there is any disagreement about the practical question of what steps to take in order to find the causes of a particular phenomenon. But would it be possible to set out anything like Mill's 'Methods' for solving moral problems? Could we even get agreement on such axioms as 'If the action caused pain intentionally, it was wrong'? Clearly this will not do as it stands, since it makes punishment wrong, and possibly even surgical operations. If we try inserting some such word as 'wantonly', or 'unjustifiably', we are no better off, since we are now saying 'If the action intentionally causes pain in circumstances where causing pain is wrong, it is wrong'. It will not even do to make it 'causing pain for the sake of causing pain', since there are at least two (very different) types of person who would disagree with us. The first type, the less reputable, but perhaps the more common, is the man who regards 'toughness', a certain insensitiveness to the pain of both himself and others, as a virtue. This applies particularly to the pain of animals: there are plenty of people who regard the opponents of bull-fighting, or other blood sports, as morally misguided: 'soft', squeamish and crankish. But it applies also to the pain of men: there are people who would be genuinely ashamed of having too much compunction about hurting others. Secondly, there are those moralists who believe that it is 'fitting' that pain should be inflicted on the wicked: not for the sake of the consequences, the probable deterrent effect, but simply on the ground that it is good in itself that good states of mind should be accompanied by pleasure, and bad states of mind by pain.[1] On the other hand, there are certainly others who regard the infliction of pain as the great, and perhaps the only, evil, justifiable, if at all, only as a means of avoiding greater pain.

Perhaps it will be said that (if not the moralist) at any rate the young tough who makes a virtue of callousness is a mere freak, like the astrologer who looks for causes by casting horoscopes, and can no more be cited as evidence of serious moral disagreement than the astrologer can be cited as evidence of serious disagreement about causal phenomena. Consider, then, the *Confessions* of Saint Augustine. It is impossible to read this book without feeling in the presence of someone who makes quite different moral assumptions from one's own. He suffers agonies

[1] 'What we perceive to be good is a condition of things in which the total pleasure enjoyed by a person in his life as a whole is proportional to his virtue similarly taken as a whole' (W. D. Ross, *The Right and the Good*, Oxford, Clarendon Press, 1930, p. 58).

of guilt over actions or dispositions which strike one as blameless or even laudable, such as a taste for literature, or the love of friends, which last he stigmatizes as 'one huge fable, one long lie; by its adulterous caressing, my mind, which lay itching in my ears, was corrupted'. (His reason is that friends die; one should fix one's affections on something eternal.) On the other hand he does not seem to feel guilty about casting off his mistress and depriving her of their illegitimate child. He did find it painful to part from her, but he seems to regard that as itself cause for guilt, as showing his unregenerate and lustful nature. Yet Augustine is not regarded as a moral freak, but (to quote his publishers) as one in whom 'every man finds a mirror for perfection' and 'who has for fifteen centuries inspired and encouraged devoted readers'. Nor can it be said that any disagreement here rests on a difference of opinion about facts: the existence of a God, or of an after-life in which certain kinds of action will be punished. For a man who did not believe that the act for which he was to be punished was wrong would feel fear, but not guilt. Moreover, it is clear that Augustine bases his opinions about what God rewards and what he punishes on his beliefs about what is good, and not vice versa.

It seems clear from these examples that there are genuine substantive moral disagreements about quite fundamental matters, and not merely meta-ethical disputes about how undisputed moral data are to be analysed. It may, indeed, be conceded that we do not usually find a systematic reversal of moral opinions, so that one man thinks good precisely what another thinks bad, and vice versa (though the moral beliefs of Augustine, when set beside those of, say, G. E. Moore, come pretty close to such a reversal: what one regards as supremely good states of mind—appreciation of beauty and love for one's friends—are condemned by the other as positively bad). There are, however, reasons, which have been set out above, why we may expect to find a fair amount of practical agreement in morals. But it is misleading to say that such disagreement as does occur is *merely* the result of placing different emphases on moral obligations which both parties acknowledge, as if this were a minor matter. Differences of opinion about which moral considerations outweigh which others are not minor: they are quite central, and make an enormous difference to men's conduct. It will be quite enough to establish our case if it is conceded that there is no generally accepted method of settling such questions: that alone would make questions of value significantly different from causal questions, or questions of fact in general.

There is, too, a second difference. At least some causal questions can be settled fairly conclusively if we reach the stage of being able to produce the effect at will by manipulating the cause. The central difficulty about moral questions is simply the absence of any practical test. It may, perhaps, be simplifying to say that there is a world of facts, outside ourselves, which serves as the final court of appeal in empirical matters; but it is certainly not wholly false. On the other hand, there does not seem to be any such final court of appeal in moral matters. It will not do, for example, to point out to Augustine that he himself describes the pleasures of friendship in moving and eloquent terms, if he persists in regarding his delight in these things as proof of original sin.

Summarizing, then:

1. It may be conceded: (*a*) that not all empirical questions can be settled by definition or are mere records of what is observed; (*b*) that some of the disputes between moral philosophers are about how moral data should be analysed, not about what constitutes moral data; (*c*) that there is in practice a fair measure of moral agreement; (*d*) that some moral disagreement arises out of disagreement about facts, and that some is about border-line cases.

2. Nevertheless, there remain some quite striking examples of disagreement over quite fundamental beliefs about substantive morality (as distinct from meta-ethics).

3. These disputed moral assertions differ from empirical assertions that go beyond what can be directly observed in that

there is no agreement about how, in principle, the dispute can be settled.

4. In some sense there is a world of facts outside ourselves which empirical assertions refer to, and by reference to which they may be settled: at least at first sight, it is doubtful whether this is true of morals.

We may, then, return to the questions which, it was suggested earlier, are the central ones for moral philosophy. Moral statements are at least sufficiently different from questions of fact to make it appear, at least at first sight, that they cannot be empirically verified. Are we, then, ever justified in making them? And what, precisely, do they mean? Have they any reference?

CHAPTER 2

END AND MEANS

Words like 'good', 'right' and 'ought' are not always used to make assertions that cannot be tested empirically. Consider the following sentences:

> A *good* burglar wears rubber-soled shoes.
> Burglars *ought* to wear rubber-soled shoes.
> Rubber-soled shoes are the *right* shoes for burglars to wear.

These three sentences all mean the same thing. Now suppose we ask: how can these statements (or this statement) be tested, on what evidence would we be prepared to assert it? The answer is quite clear. The test is whether burglars who wear rubber-soled shoes are less frequently caught than those who do not. Now obviously this is a matter of observation and experience. It would be quite easy for the Burglars' Association or the Rubbergrowers' Federation or both of them together to devise a series of experiments which would test this.

What is the connection between 'A good burglar wears rubber-soled shoes' and 'Burglars who wear rubber-soled shoes are hard to catch'? It is at least a good deal like the relation between 'He could not have avoided punishment without lying' and 'Lying was necessary to avoid punishment'. 'A burglar who does not get caught' is part of the meaning of 'a good burglar'. This is not all that is meant: a burglar who never got caught but who never (or seldom) got away with anything worth having would not be a good burglar. But neither would a burglar who managed to get the valuables out of the safe but was usually caught before he escaped with them. A good burglar, in fact, is an efficient burglar. This statement is analytic: 'good' here means 'efficient'. And to be efficient is to achieve the purposes, or the ends, at which you aim. A good burglar, then, is one who achieves the purposes of a burglar.

These are, I suppose, the two I have mentioned: to get his hands on the goods and to avoid getting caught.

All these are matters of observation. We can test by observation whether burglars who wear rubber-soled shoes do, on the whole, avoid capture; we can find out by observation (perhaps by some kind of Gallup poll, perhaps simply by watching them) what the purposes of burglars are. If a burglar tried to get caught, like the one in *Heartbreak House*, his being caught would not prevent him from being a good burglar.

If, then, 'good' means 'efficient' then any statement to the effect that something is good is an empirical statement. But does 'good' always mean 'efficient'? Very often, no doubt, it does. A good suitcase is a suitcase which is efficient in carrying out the purposes for which suitcases are used. This is also true of a good motor-car, a good knife, a good mattress, etc., etc. And we can rephrase all these statements so as to use 'right' or 'ought' instead of 'good'. A good suitcase is the right suitcase or the one you ought to use.

We have been considering the words 'good', 'right' and 'ought', however, only because these are usually thought of as the typical terms used in making statements about morals. But the statements we have been considering would not usually be regarded as moral statements at all. A good burglar, it would be said, is not a good man. To say this is to raise a moral issue, whereas in talking about 'a good burglar' hitherto we have been avoiding moral issues. It looks, then, as if there may be moral and non-moral uses of the word 'good'. To talk about a good man is to use the word in the moral sense; to talk about a good burglar is not. And it may be that it is only in the non-moral uses that 'good' is an empirical term.

Is a good man one who is efficient in achieving the purposes that he actually has? Most people would not say so. They would add that he needs to aim at the right purposes, good purposes, the purposes he ought to have, before he can be regarded as a good man. Indeed many people would say that provided he does have the right purposes and does at least try to attain them, he is a good man even if he is not successful.

It looks, then, as if to be good in the non-moral sense is to be efficient in attaining the purposes you actually have, or the purposes that someone else has for you (if you are a suitcase, a knife, a mattress, a private in the army, or indeed a subordinate of any kind); to be good in the moral sense is to be diligent in attaining the purposes you ought to have. But what is meant by 'the purposes you ought to have'? Of course one might say 'A burglar ought to try to avoid getting caught'. Here we are talking about a purpose that a burglar ought to have. But if we ask why he ought to have this aim, the answer is obvious. He ought to aim at avoiding capture because if he is caught he will probably go to prison and he does not want to go to prison. In other words, the aim or end we say he ought to have turns out to be a means to a further end (avoiding prison) which he already has. So here again it is simply a question of attaining a purpose he actually has. If we say, however, that a small boy ought to be kind to his little brother, we do not mean that this is a means to some further end which he actually has, such as being rewarded by his parents. We are inclined to say that he ought to be kind whether this is a means to any further end or not.

The implication seems to be that there are some ends that men ought to pursue, not as means to further ends but simply for their own sake. If we accept this the distinction between the moral and the non-moral uses of 'good' may be regarded as a distinction between 'good as a means' and 'good as an end'. To say that something is good as a means is to make an empirical statement, but to say that it is good as an end is not.

It may be as well to illustrate this. Suppose an economist is asked whether the forty-hour week is a good thing or not. Simplifying a little, we may say that for him this question amounts to: Does the forty-hour week lead to an increase in production or not? Is the increase in production which one might expect to result from longer hours of work counteracted by increased fatigue and dissatisfaction among the workers? Now this is clearly an empirical question. It can be answered by examining the statistics of production of industries in which a forty-hour week is worked and comparing them with the statistics of production in industries in which longer hours are worked. Of course there may be difficulties about this in practice. Accurate statistics may not be available. Again, it may be that industries in which the hours of work are short are also those in which there is more efficient machinery and further observations will have to be made in order to determine the effect of this. But whatever the practical difficulties may be, at least it is quite clear what we are trying to decide and what kind of evidence would enable us to decide it.

Again, suppose an individual worker is asked whether from his point of view (not the economist's point of view) the forty-hour week is a good thing or not. For him this will be quite a different question. It will be whether the forty-hour week is an efficient means to his ends, the ends he happens to have; and maximum production may not be one of these. Let us suppose that he is a keen yachtsman and that his aim is to have as much time as possible to spend in his boat. For him, then, the question is: Will the forty-hour week give me more time to spend on the harbour? And this is obviously an empirical question. Of course the answer to it may be more complex than one might expect. It may turn out, for example, that the forty-hour week reduces production and so raises prices, with the result that he finds that he has to discover some way of supplementing his income. This may mean that he has to spend his spare time doing odd jobs in someone else's garden, say, instead of in yachting. But whatever the answer may be, the question is a clear one and we know on what kind of evidence we would answer it one way or the other.

Both these questions, then, are questions about means to a given end and both are empirical. But now let us suppose that someone (from the pulpit perhaps, or in a newspaper editorial) denounces the forty-hour week on the grounds that it shows the slothfulness, the degeneracy and the lack of moral fibre of our times. What would this mean? There does not seem to be any question here of means and ends. It is not suggested that the forty-hour week prevents the modern Australian from attaining some ends which he has. The suggestion is rather that the ends he does pursue are the wrong ones, ones he ought not to pursue. Now how could this be established, what sort of observation would enable us to decide this question? By what possible observation can we tell whether a given individual ought to pursue an end which he does not pursue?

There is, then, at least a case for saying that the questions of value discussed in the first chapter are questions about what things are good as ends, or what ends men ought to pursue. This distinction between ends and means, however, has been questioned by some philosophers. It will therefore be necessary to discuss it further.

Suppose I have to go from Sydney to Melbourne next week. I ask myself: How shall I go? By train or 'plane, boat or bus? At first sight, this looks like a simple means–end problem. The end (getting to Melbourne) is given, and I am asking myself which is the most efficient means to this end.

But what does 'efficient' mean here? All these are efficient in that they will (almost certainly) get me to Melbourne. If I knew that one train in four broke down and failed to complete the journey, I might say that this was not an efficient means of transport, meaning by this that there was quite a high chance of my end not being attained. And I do in fact reject, indeed I simply do not consider, some possible means of getting to Melbourne for this reason. I could, no doubt, try to swim or row there; but (apart from any other consideration) I am not a strong enough swimmer or oarsman to be able to do this successfully. But I feel quite confident that 'plane, train, boat or bus would all get me there. In choosing between them, I do not ask myself: Which is most likely to get me there? What I do ask is: Which is most comfortable? Which is quickest? Which costs least?

This suggests that I have at least three other ends in mind besides getting to Melbourne: avoiding discomfort, saving time and saving money. All these admit of degree: I can be more or less comfortable, save more or less time and money, whereas I either get to Melbourne or I do not. There is, then, a very clear meaning to the question: Is train, 'plane, bus or boat *more* efficient in these three respects?

Is it true that these three are all ends rather than means? Avoiding discomfort fairly obviously is an end. If someone were to ask us why we try to be comfortable, we should regard this as a curious question; and, if pressed for an answer, we should probably say something like: 'Well, I just like being comfortable.' There is, however, a verbal difficulty here. To be comfortable is to be in a state of body which one finds pleasant: that is what 'comfortable' means. It is, then, an analytic proposition that one likes being comfortable. Like most analytic propositions, however, this rests on a synthetic one: that men find some physical states pleasant and others unpleasant. Different men may find different physical states pleasant: I may be quite comfortable on a chair which causes you acute discomfort. But one of my ends is the attaining of those physical states which I do find pleasant.

Saving time is not an end in quite the same sense. Suppose I find that the 'plane will get me to Melbourne very quickly; but that, as a result, I shall arrive there three or four hours before the time of my appointment, with nothing to do but walk about the streets. I may decide that I would rather spend the time in the train, reading a book. Saving time is clearly not an end in itself; we usually take it to be so only because we take it for granted that the time saved can be spent on activities which we find pleasant. Much the same can be said about saving money. The money is of no use to me unless there are things I can spend it on: things that I would enjoy having. Saving time and saving money, we may say, are themselves means to further ends. So far as our example goes, it looks as if we have not really come to an end, as distinct from a means, until we can say: 'I do that just because I like it, find it pleasant; I do it for its own sake, not for the sake of its consequences.'

If this is what we mean by an end, then getting to Melbourne is not an end, any more than saving time or money. We have supposed that I want to go to Melbourne in order to keep an appointment, and this is presumably itself a means to some further end.

How does it come about that what we at first took to be ends turn out not to be? The answer is quite simple. Once we have made up our minds to do something, we regard that thing as an end. Once I have decided to go to Melbourne, getting to Melbourne becomes an end for me, and the only further question is: 'how shall I attain this end?' Similarly, once I have decided to go by train (say) getting to the train becomes an end for me, and the next question is about the most efficient means to *that* end. (By bus or taxi to the station?) But, when I have not yet made up my mind whether or not to do some particular thing, I regard it as a means: I ask myself what further ends it will attain. Going by train and going by 'plane both attain the end of getting me to Melbourne. I can settle the question between them only by considering further ends, such as the saving of time or money. These are ends for me because I have, like most people, already adopted a rule of saving time (at least on journeys and the like) and money whenever I can do so without sacrificing some other end that I regard as more important. But I have decided to treat saving time and money as ends because I have learned from experience that I can generally use the time or the money in ways which, for one reason or another, I think desirable.

The distinction between end and means, then, is relative to a decision. The course of action becomes an end once I have decided to try to follow it. Very often I decide to follow it because it is a means to some further end. But this is not always true: sometimes my reason is just that I like doing this kind of thing. This gives us a slightly different sense of 'end' and 'means'. We can say that something is an end (or 'an ultimate end') for me when my reason for choosing it is just that I like it, or find it pleasant. The term 'ultimate means' is not often used, but we could use it to refer to an activity (like getting to Melbourne in my example) which, though an end relatively to some other activities, is aimed at by me, not because I find it pleasant, but because I find its consequences pleasant. The terms 'good in itself' or 'good as a means' are often used for what I have called 'ultimate end' and 'ultimate means'. So are 'intrinsically good' and 'instrumentally good'.

Some philosophers have attacked the whole end–means distinction. There are, I think, these reasons for doing so:

1. As we have seen, the same activity may be an end from one point of view and a means from another. Consequently, it is argued, the distinction between good-as-a-means and good-as-an-end is not the absolute one that moral philosophers have often taken it to be.

This objection loses its force once we realize that we are thinking of what is ultimately an end and ultimately a means: that is, that the question 'Is it good as a means or as an end?' amounts to 'Do you aim at it because you like it or because you like its consequences?'

2. The same activity may, however, be pursued for both reasons. A man may walk to his office every morning both because he wants to get there and because he enjoys walking.

This is not an objection to the distinction. It is only an objection to taking too simple a view of the distinction: to treating it as if every objective were either good-as-a-means or good-as-an-end and never both.

3. The same activity may be a means for one man and an end for another. You may walk to your office because, although you dislike walking, you want to get there and have no other means of transport; I may decide to accompany you, even though this will take me out of my way, because I enjoy walking.

This, too, is not an objection to the distinction between means and ends. It is an objection to talking about good-as-a-means and good-as-an-end as if these were qualities of things and not relative to people.

4. We may come to regard something as good-in-itself because it is good-as-a-means. The classic example, which goes back at least to Gay and Hartley, is the miser who desires money for its own sake. Presumably he does so only because he originally desired it as a means. Moreover, if money lost its exchange value, if it ceased to be a means by which other goods could be obtained, the miser would no longer want it, even though he does not in fact use it to obtain those goods.

This does not in itself vitiate the distinction, though it does suggest that the psychological connection between wanting something as a means and wanting it for its own sake may be more complex than appears at first sight. This objection does, however, lead on to the next.

5. If pressed, a man might often be quite at a loss to say whether he wanted something as a means or as an end. The truth is that we pursue a large number of different objectives, which are related to one another in various ways. We try to make money, for example, partly because we do consciously want the things that money can buy; partly because we want the sense of security and of power that comes from knowing that we have money; partly because having a profession or trade is part of the accepted pattern of life in our culture, and we would feel uneasy if we stepped outside that pattern. It is quite misleading to consider any one activity in isolation, as if it had to be pursued either for its own sake or for the sake of some definite consequence or set of consequences. This is misleading, not only because our motives are mixed, but also because no one of these motives can be properly understood if it is considered out of relation to the others, and to the whole pattern of life of which they form part. One might say that the only thing valued for its own sake is just this pattern of life as a whole; but this too would be misleading, for in fact we are not conscious of any objective so remote from our everyday concerns as a pattern of life.

This objection is, I believe, more cogent than the others. It should make us consider what exactly we are asking when we ask: Do I pursue this objective for its own sake or for the sake of its consequences? We may be asking: What is my conscious motive? And here the answer may well be that I pursue this objective out of habit, or because it is the custom, without ever asking myself whether I value it or its consequences. We may be asking: Would I in fact pursue it if it did not have the consequences it does have? And this is not only a question to which I may not know the answer, but one to which the answer may be quite complex. It may be, for example, that the custom of pursuing it would persist for some generations, and would then gradually die out. Finally, we may be asking, not: Why do I in fact pursue this objective? but: How would I justify its pursuit, if pressed to do so? And it may be that, if this question were put to me, I would have no idea how to answer it.

When all this has been said, the means–end distinction remains a useful one, provided we understand exactly how it is being used. We do justify some of our activities to ourselves by reference to their consequences. This kind of justification is clearly incomplete, because it invites a further question: Why aim at these consequences in particular? The difficulty of answering this kind of question is the problem that we have so far been considering.

CHAPTER 3

TYPES OF MORAL THEORY

The questions moral philosophers have to answer are:

1. What precisely is being said when we claim that somebody ought to do something or that something is good as an end?

2. How can such assertions be justified if they are challenged?

These questions arise because of the differences that have been detected between statements about value and statements of fact or empirical statements. Empirical statements can be both explicated and justified by referring to something that can be observed. The peculiarity of moral statements is just that with them this procedure does not work.

It is quite possible to regard the history of moral philosophy as essentially a series of attempts to solve this problem, which in one form or another has always engaged the attention of philosophers. In particular, we may distinguish between the naturalist and the non-naturalist solutions.

The naturalist tries to bridge the gap between 'ought' and 'is' by explaining away the differences that have been pointed out. As we have seen, 'ought' can be reduced to 'is' easily enough provided that we take some end for granted. 'Burglars ought to wear rubber-soled shoes' may be readily translated 'Wearing rubber-soled shoes is an efficient means of avoiding capture'. Provided that we do not call into question the purposes that the burglar actually has, all our prescriptions can be regarded as assertions about means to a given end and these are empirical statements like any other. The naturalist explains that all moral statements do in fact have an implicit reference to some end which is not questioned. It is not questioned simply because it is a universal end which all men do in fact have. It is only because men have not realized this that the whole problem has arisen. Once we do realize it, the central problem of moral philosophy can be quite easily solved. For example, one widely held naturalist view is the hedonist one that moral principles are simply rules about how to obtain as much pleasure as possible. Pleasure is not, however, the only end that has been put forward. It is sometimes said that the end is simply keeping society together: preventing it from falling to pieces, dissolving into anarchy. Moral principles, on this view, are the rules which men must follow if they are to live together harmoniously and co-operate in society. Or again, there was a view, popular in the nineteenth century as a result of the first impact of Darwinian views on evolution and not quite dead today, that moral principles are rules about how to secure the survival of the species, that is, the human race. What all such theories have in common is that they reduce all ought-statements, except one, to empirical statements about the most efficient means of achieving the given end. The one ought-statement left unresolved is: ought we to pursue pleasure (or social cohesion or the survival of mankind)? This question, the naturalist claims, is, properly considered, a meaningless one. It is meaningless just because, whether we realize it or not, moral judgements do in fact implicitly assume this end.

The non-naturalist, on the other hand, denies that moral statements can be reduced to statements about what is the case. He is quite prepared to accept the view that moral statements are not empirical. He does not, however, regard this as anything to worry about, or even to puzzle over. To deny that moral statements are empirical is not for him to deny that they are factual. There are, he claims, facts which are not detected by the senses and which cannot be established by the method of observation, but which are none the less real and important. Moral statements express such facts. That it is wrong to cause unnecessary suffering to others, for example, is as much a fact as that grass is green. It is not a fact that we know by means of our senses but we do know it, nevertheless, and no sane man will dispute it. The non-naturalist will probably go on to say that things have not merely sensible qualities like colour which may be detected by means of the senses, but also non-natural qualities like rightness or wrongness, goodness or badness, which are detected not by means of the senses but in some other way. Some non-naturalists have regarded reason as the means by which we obtain knowledge of such non-natural qualities.

There is a third possible solution to our problem which has been put forward by some philosophers in comparatively recent times and which, though it was touched on in the first chapter, needs fuller treatment here. Non-naturalists have often supported their case by pointing out that there are non-moral statements which cannot be established empirically and yet which are quite certainly true. Favourite examples are the axioms of logic or of mathematics: for example, that any assertion is either true or false, or that two straight lines cannot enclose a space. We do not learn these things by using our eyes and ears: it is rather that reason enables us to see that they must be true. These non-naturalists, whom we may call rationalists, go on to argue that major premises in moral reasoning are apparent to reason in exactly the same way. Many logicians and mathematicians, however, no longer claim that their axioms are self-evident truths of reason or even that they are truths at all. They are, it is claimed, rather postulates which are assumed simply for the sake of the resulting system. We are quite at liberty, if we like and if we can, to construct a geometry in which two straight lines do enclose a space, or a logic in which some propositions are neither true nor false.

If we adopt this position we may need to modify our view of empirical statements also. It is not, after all, quite true that all empirical statements can be established by reference simply to the evidence of our senses. Plainly we do need the assumptions made in logic and perhaps in geometry as well. If on the evidence of sight I say that grass is green I am after all assuming that grass cannot be both green and not green at the same time. It is only within a framework of assumptions of this kind that the appeal to the senses does enable us to establish empirical propositions. If we did adopt an alternative logic, or even an alternative geometry, we might find the evidence of our senses pointing to quite different conclusions.

Arguing along these lines, this third group of philosophers claims, as we have already seen, that there is after all no important difference between moral statements and empirical ones. Empirical reasoning, like moral reasoning, can only get started if we assume certain major premises that cannot themselves be proved. This view differs from the naturalist one in that it is not claimed that the major premises of moral reasoning are themselves, when properly understood, empirical statements. It differs from the non-naturalist view in that it does not claim that these major premises are statements of self-evident moral facts. Both moral and empirical reasoning, these philosophers claim, start from certain postulates or assumptions which are not facts but which are in some sense written into the rules of the language which we use. Consequently they resemble the naturalists in denying any sharp cleavage between ought-statements and is-statements but resemble the non-naturalists in that they deny that moral statements can be reduced to empirical ones. The language of morals is a different language from the language of empirical statements: it makes different assumptions; but there is no more difficulty about the one kind of language than the other.

Each of these three solutions of our problem will now be expounded in more detail.

CHAPTER 4

NATURALISM

Consider a plant growing in a rather dark place: it stretches out towards the sun. We may feel inclined to say that the plant wants to reach the sunlight; but no one is likely to take this literally. We have no doubt that the behaviour of the plant can be fully explained in terms of biochemical processes. Now suppose the plant to be endowed with consciousness: this will make no difference to the biochemical processes, which go on exactly as before. Nor need we suppose that the plant is conscious of these processes as such, any more than we are conscious of the circulation of the blood. We might expect the plant to feel a kind of restlessness, perhaps a specific desire for sunshine. It would not surprise us if the plant (supposing it to have the gift of speech) were to say that sunshine is good and that cold and darkness are bad.

In living organisms there is a gradation from the complete lack of consciousness of plants to the relatively full consciousness of man. The biochemical processes of course go on, *mutatis mutandis*, as in the plant; they are reflected in consciousness as desires. For example, the animal is not aware of contractions in his stomach: what he is aware of is a feeling of hunger. In man these desires become purposes: that is to say, a man may know just what will gratify the desire and may consciously plan the steps necessary to attain it.

The biochemical processes that lead to food seeking are reflected in consciousness as the feeling we call hunger. Similarly, the impulse to reach out towards food which is part of the same biological process will be reflected in consciousness by the belief that food is good.

This is a typical naturalist explanation of moral terms. It was put forward in very much this form by Thomas Hobbes, who is a thorough-going and clear-headed naturalist. According to

Hobbes, animals (including men) have two basic responses to their environment: one is to reach out towards an external object, the other is to shrink back from it. We may imagine a very simple organism endowed with just these two responses: perhaps, a kind of jelly-fish floating in the sea. Some of the organisms around it constitute its food, and these it seizes; others prey upon it, and from these it retreats. According to Hobbes, the whole complex emotional life of man is built on these two kinds of response, which he calls appetites (seekings towards) and aversions (turnings away from) respectively. Some modern psychologists talk of adient and avoidant responses, which would seem to be exactly the same. Hobbes thinks that any emotion can be analysed as one of these, plus a belief about a matter of fact. For example, he defines hope as an appetite accompanied by the belief that the object of the appetite is likely to be attained. Fear is an aversion, together with the belief that the object of the aversion is likely to cause one injury. The generic term for both appetites and aversions is 'endeavour'. As with the jelly-fish, men have instinctive appetites and aversions for certain objects in their environment; the process of association, or what modern psychologists have called 'conditioning', enables these reactions to be transferred to other objects. Consequently the emotions and desires of men may become highly complex as the result of experience. Moreover, as men's experiences differ, they may come to feel desire for very different objects.

Once this has been understood, Hobbes thinks, the mystery that has surrounded the meaning of moral terms is completely dispelled: we no longer need to regard 'goodness' and 'badness', 'rightness' and 'wrongness', as the names of mysterious qualities which cannot be detected by the senses but which somehow attach themselves to objects or actions. We can understand how terms like 'good' and 'bad' arise quite naturally to express the attitudes which men feel for the objects of their appetites and aversions. In Hobbes's own words:

but whatsoever is the object of any man's Appetite or Desire; that is it which he for his part calleth Good; and the object of his Hate, and Aversion, Evill...For these words...are ever used with relation to the person that useth them; there being nothing simply and absolutely so; nor any common Rule of Good and Evill to be taken from the nature of the objects themselves.[1]

On this view, to say that something is good as a means is to say that it will lead to the gratification of a desire. To say that something is good as an end is to say that it is itself the object of a desire. That something is a means to the gratification of desire is a question of fact in the same way as that something is itself the object of desire is a question of fact: ultimately a biological fact. Consequently Hobbes regards himself as having reduced moral questions to empirical ones.

But how, it may be asked, does this meet the logical point that moral reasoning must begin with a major premise that is itself a moral statement? It is not hard to see how Hobbes would answer this. If we take the major premise to be 'Whatever is the object of a desire is good' this is, according to Hobbes, an analytic proposition; 'good' just means 'object of desire'. It may be objected that this is simply untrue. We sometimes think that the object of a given desire is not good and in saying this we do not seem to be contradicting ourselves. We may also doubt whether we ought always to gratify our desires. Hobbes would reply, I think, that desires may conflict: consequently the same thing may be good (in so far as it is the object of one desire) and at the same time bad (in so far as it is a hindrance to another desire). If the second desire is stronger than the first then we will regard the thing in question as on the whole bad. Similarly, we may say that we ought not to gratify the first desire, simply because this will mean thwarting the second desire. He would, however, deny that it makes sense to say that the object of a desire is not good unless it gets in the way of some other desire. It does not make sense, either, to say that desires as such ought not to be gratified. To say that we ought to do something is ultimately just to express a desire to do that thing.

[1] *Leviathan*, Book I, ch. 6.

The whole matter is complicated, however, not merely by the conflict of desires within the breast of the individual, but also by the fact that the desires of different men conflict. Consequently what Hobbes calls 'a state of nature', in which each man seeks to gratify his own desires without taking account of his neighbours', is one of mutual suspicion and hostility. But this is not a good state: that is to say, it is not one in which any man has much chance of gratifying many of his desires. So far as they realized this, men in such a state would be impelled to find some expedient for ending it. As it happens they have found such an expedient: it is the device of law and order, the adoption of certain rules which each man obeys on condition that his fellows obey them too. Whether or not this is the actual historical origin of society it is, Hobbes thinks, its underlying *raison d'être*.

This means that, in effect, Hobbes has a two-level analysis of morality, which is a good deal more subtle than his critics usually acknowledge. At one level morality can be thought of as just those rules which societies adopt in order to prevent a collapse into anarchy, the state of nature in which every man's hand is against every other man's hand. It is simply a sociological fact that such rules are necessary if a society is to function smoothly. Since this is so, any society will see to it that these rules are inculcated in its members and, in particular, in each new generation of children. The moral feelings of any individual are the result of this process of indoctrination. At this level we may define morality as the rules necessary to keep society together. To say that one ought to do X is just to say that X is required by these rules. At this level it hardly makes sense to ask whether we ought to try to prevent society from collapsing. It is only within a context in which societies frame rules for this purpose that moral terms come to be used and to acquire their meaning. Outside such a context the notion of being *obliged* to do something does not arise. Human beings do, as a simple matter of fact, have feelings of obligation, duty and the like. It is the principles which express these feelings that they use as the major premises in their reasoning about morals. We need not suppose that these major premises represent an intuitive knowledge of mysterious non-empirical facts: there is a simple sociological explanation for their occurrence.

This explains what moral principles are and how it is that men come to adopt them and to regulate their conduct by them. At this level 'I ought to do X' means 'X follows from one of the socially acquired principles by which I regulate my life and whose ultimate justification is the preservation of society'. At this level the question 'Ought I to try to prevent society from collapsing?' hardly makes sense, since the word 'ought' arises only as an expression of the feelings engendered by the process of social conditioning already described. At another level, however, this question clearly does make sense. If I break these social rules my conscience will prick me and I will feel guilt and remorse. But it is possible, if I have enough will power, to resist the promptings of conscience: I can, accordingly, ask myself whether I ought not to resist them. I am not now asking 'is what my conscience tells me in accordance with what my conscience tells me?' but 'is there any sound reason for subordinating all my other desires to these socially engendered ones?'

Here we reach the second level of Hobbes's analysis. His answer to our question is simply that the social rules are necessary if society is not to collapse and that if society does collapse I shall have very little chance of gratifying any of my desires. The ultimate appeal, then, is to self-interest: that is, to the gratification of as many desires as possible. And to ask 'ought I to gratify my desires?' is, for Hobbes, strictly meaningless. This account of morality (which admittedly is an elaboration of what Hobbes actually says, though it does not, I think, go beyond what Hobbes meant)[1] does provide Hobbes with answers to most of the criticisms brought against him. (I

---

[1] This whole interpretation of Hobbes has been disputed. I believe it to be correct, but anyone who disagrees is invited simply to consider this account as referring to a possible meta-ethical theory, and to ignore the attribution to Hobbes.

leave open the question whether these answers are finally convincing.) It explains, for example, why our moral feelings often seem to run counter to our desires, and why it is that the moral point of view seems to be that of the impartial observer rather than that of self-interest. To the extent that social rules are not impartial, men will be stirred to revolt against them and the society will be torn by dissension, which it is the whole object of morality to avoid.

Nevertheless, the contention that morality is ultimately based on self-interest roused, and still rouses, considerable opposition. It is worth noticing why there is a strong case for it. The naturalist thesis requires that the ultimate major premise of moral reasoning be an analytic proposition: one that is true by definition. Although it may not seem so at first sight, such propositions as 'One ought to do what one most desires to do' or 'One ought to do whatever gives one most pleasure in the long run' fulfil this requirement much better than 'One ought to do one's duty' or 'One ought to do what one's conscience commands'. For the question 'Why bother about duty?' is a perfectly sensible one which does indeed force itself upon anyone with an alert mind. 'Why bother about doing what you want to do?' does not seem to be sensible. It may be objected that 'what I want to do' and 'what I ought to do' are quite distinct concepts. This point will be discussed when we come to consider what G. E. Moore called 'the naturalistic fallacy'. The point at the moment is that if we are looking for a final and unanswerable reason for action, 'I did it because I wanted to' provides it. 'Why did you want to do that?' (what about it made you want to do it?) does of course make sense, but 'why do you do what you want to do?' does not. It is this that makes plausible the Hobbist thesis that moral terms are, when properly understood, simply a means of expressing our attitude to what we desire. If moral reasoning is reasoning about means to given ends, requiring as an ultimate first premise 'X is the end to be chosen', there is a strong case for saying that this is equivalent to 'when everything has been taken into consideration, including the facts of social life and my need for the co-operation and esteem of my fellow men, *X* is what I most want'.

In spite of this, many naturalists have not been satisfied with self-interest as the ultimate basis of morality. The development of naturalist theories of ethics in the century or so after Hobbes is instructive, because it illustrates the main variants of naturalism. Shaftesbury, Butler and Hutcheson are quite prepared to agree with Hobbes that moral terms arise as the expression of deep-seated, instinctive human feelings. But, they argue, Hobbes is taking a very narrow and one-sided view of human nature: he takes account only of a particular set of human feelings: those which are summed up as the urge for self-preservation. Self-interest is a slightly wider term than self-preservation and takes in a few more human motives, but, they claim, there is more in human nature than simply self-interest. It is true that men do find themselves, for example, shrinking from pain, seeking food and so on. But they also find themselves, for example, shrinking from the pain of others. Any normal person seeing a baby, let us say, attacked by a savage dog would certainly feel distressed and would have an impulse to save the baby. This would hardly seem to spring from an instinct of *self*-preservation; but it seems to be, none the less, a deep-rooted human feeling: to be part of human nature. We need, then, to make a distinction between those feelings which are grouped together under the name of self-interest and feelings of this second kind. We may call these, if we like, benevolent feelings as distinct from interested ones. Benevolence, these moralists insist, is as much a part of human nature as self-interest.

Once this distinction has been made, there are grounds for questioning Hobbes's contention that moral principles are simply maxims about how to attain the ends set before us by self-interest. It is true that we do adopt principles which have this purpose. There is the saying, for example, that every man is either a fool or his own doctor by forty. That is to say, a sensible man will in time find by experience which way of life enables him to avoid illness and suffering. This is very much the way that, according to Hobbes, moral principles arise. A moral code is just a set of prescriptions for a way of life which will lead to the gratification of our desires and so the avoidance of suffering. But, it may be objected, we would not usually call the rules which the prudent man of forty lays down for himself a moral code or a set of moral principles. Suppose he were to say to us: 'Well, my morality is very simple. I make it a rule never to eat cheese late at night, always to keep my feet dry and to wear heavy underwear in winter.' We would certainly feel that this was not a morality. And even if he were to say (and this, of course, is much closer to what Hobbes actually says): 'I make it a rule never to hit a man bigger than myself, or indeed one smaller than myself either, because he may have friends, or a revolver; and I always keep promises, because, if you don't, you will always get found out in the end' —even if he were to say this, we would still be doubtful about calling these rules moral ones. They come closer, perhaps, to being moral rules than the first set; but we would probably feel that they are essentially, like the first ones, rules of prudence and not moral principles at all.

On this view, then, Hobbes is right in analysing moral terms as the expression of a deep-seated human instinct. He is wrong, however, in supposing that instinct to be self-interest. There is another human instinct, equally deep-seated: benevolence. It is this instinct that moral terms express. 'X is right' is to be analysed as 'X is a means of attaining the ends set before me by my benevolent instincts'. To say that I do something for its own sake or as an end in itself may not be to say that I do it because I like it. It may be that I do it because somebody else likes it. That too is a final reason for action. The point may be put in this way, even by philosophers who dislike the eighteenth-century language of 'human nature' and 'human instinct'. Thus a modern writer, Professor Baier, distinguishes between different types of 'good reason' for an action. One is that 'I enjoy it'; another is that 'someone else enjoys it'.

We are now, however, faced with a difficulty. Hobbes and his followers would say that self-interest is the sole human motive and that ultimately all other motives, including benevolence, can be reduced to it. If human beings have ultimately only one goal and moral rules tell us how to attain that goal, it is easy to see why moral principles should be obeyed. If we have two basic instincts, however, self-interest and benevolence, giving rise to two sets of principles, rules of prudence and moral principles, then how do we choose between them when they conflict? According to the naturalist 'I ought to do X' can be analysed as 'Doing X is a means of gratifying an instinctive urge'. It would follow that if there are two fundamental instincts there are two types of 'ought': the ought of self-interest and the ought of benevolence. 'I ought to do X' will mean either 'X is in my interest' or 'I am prompted to do X by feelings of benevolence'.

The difficulty is that most moralists want to say that we ought to follow moral principles rather than principles of self-interest when these conflict. What could this mean on a naturalist analysis of 'ought'? It is clear that if ought-statements express either the instinct of self-interest or the instinct of benevolence, then 'I ought to do X' cannot give us a reason for preferring one of these to the other.

One solution is to say that there is yet a third instinct which has the special function of enabling us to choose between the other two. This instinct may be called 'conscience' or 'the moral sense'. This gives us a third sense of 'ought' and it is this that is the distinctively moral sense. On this view, to say that I ought to prefer benevolence to self-interest when they conflict is to say that I have an instinctive feeling of approval for benevolent actions as distinct from interested ones. This too is just a fact of human nature. These instinctive feelings of approval and disapproval are referred to collectively by Hutcheson as 'the moral sense'. It just is a fact that men have these feelings: that we find ourselves approving of some kinds of actions and disapproving of others. It is these feelings, and not self-interest or benevolence, that we express when we use moral terms. (In saying this Hutcheson is departing somewhat from Butler's view, which was that conscience is indeed a third instinct, but is an instinctive tendency to judge actions according to certain rules such as that lying is wrong.)

Hutcheson's view may be made clear by comparing the moral sense with the sense of beauty, which he also regards as part of human nature. According to him, men find themselves reacting instinctively to certain sights and sounds. Confronted with a painting, a sunset or a symphony, men have certain quite distinctive feelings which they express by talking about beauty. It is a mistake, however, to suppose that beauty is the name of a mysterious non-natural quality residing in these things. A thing is beautiful because it has certain perfectly natural qualities of symmetry and proportion. To call it beautiful is to say that it has those qualities and is, at the same time, to express the instinctive feelings which we have for anything with those qualities. In exactly the same way, to say that a thing is good or that an action is right is to say that it has certain natural qualities and is, at the same time, to express an instinctive feeling of approval for those qualities. The way to discover what qualities rouse aesthetic emotions is to analyse the different things we regard as beautiful and try to discover what characteristics are common and peculiar to them. This is the task of aesthetics. (Hutcheson's own aesthetic theory is that beauty consists in the utmost possible uniformity together with the utmost possible variety.) In the same way we may look for the characteristics which are common and peculiar to the things for which we feel moral approval. Hutcheson's answer here is that we approve of those actions which show evidence of benevolent intention. At the moment we are not concerned with the details of Hutcheson's moral theory, but with the general pattern of his analysis of moral statements. This analysis may be stated as follows:

A moral statement, such as 'X is good', is true if:

1. X has certain natural characteristics.
2. Those characteristics evoke certain feelings (pro-attitudes

as some more recent philosophers have called them) in the speaker and consequently (human beings being alike in this respect) in all or most men.

This has been put in a sufficiently general form to serve as a statement of the naturalist position in general. It would apply, for example, to Hobbes as well as to Hutcheson and the other members of the moral sense school.

The naturalist is often taken to be making the first of these two assertions, but not the second. Consequently it is quite usual to distinguish naturalism from subjectivism: subjectivism is the view that moral terms either state or express the feelings of the speaker, or perhaps of some group of men which may or may not include the speaker, such as members of a given community or the majority of mankind. It is useful to distinguish between these two elements in the position outlined above. To use the term 'naturalist', however, in this way is to set up a man of straw and may lead us to underestimate the strength of the traditional naturalist theory. The great traditional naturalists in ethics, such as Hobbes, Hutcheson or Hume, were certainly subjectivists as well.

There is, however, one subjectivist position which differs in one important respect from the position outlined above. It may certainly be doubted whether men always do approve of the same things: whether feelings of approval are always evoked by the same natural characteristics. Both Hutcheson and Hume are at some pains to show that men do, at bottom, have the same moral sense. Their arguments are not, however, conclusive. A good many subjectivists would agree with the analysis given above, except that they would rewrite (2) to omit the reference to all or most men.

Two others questions have been much discussed by recent writers on moral philosophy. It may be doubted whether 'X is good' is precisely equivalent to 'I have feelings of approval for X', since the speaker may not (consciously) mean this in the least: he may believe, for example, that the term 'good' refers to a non-natural quality. This difficulty may be met by saying that moral terms *express* such feelings rather than state that the speaker has them; since our utterances often express feelings of which we are not conscious. Secondly, it may be doubted whether (1) is part of the *meaning* of 'X is good'. No doubt I will not say that X is good unless X does in fact have some natural characteristics which rouse feelings of approval in me, but I may not know what these characteristics are, and I may not consciously be asserting (1). Consequently, some philosophers have preferred to say that (1) is in some sense implied by 'X is good', but is not part of its meaning. It is for this reason that I have stated the naturalist analysis, not in terms of the meaning of moral statements, but as an account of the conditions which must hold if moral statements are true. Probably, however, the traditional naturalists did regard this analysis as an explication of the meaning of moral terms.

When these points have been made, however, it is clear that the modern philosophers who put them forward do not seriously disagree with the naturalist reduction of ought-statements to is-statements. Men have feelings of approval, or pro-attitudes: moral statements arise as an expression of these feelings. This is not essentially different from what Hobbes, or any of his naturalist successors, had said.

CHAPTER 5

INTUITIONISM AND RATIONALISM

So far I have called the view that moral terms refer to non-empirical qualities or relations simply 'non-naturalism'. But I have also mentioned a third view, which, so far as it is distinguished from naturalism, is presumably also a non-naturalist one. To avoid confusion I shall, in this chapter, use 'intuitionism' or 'rationalism' for what I earlier called 'non-naturalism'. (The differences between intuitionism and rationalism are not relevant at this point.) Actually, I shall argue a little later that the third position can be interpreted as either a naturalist or a non-naturalist one, so that it does not really provide a third solution to the is–ought problem. If this is accepted, it is convenient to use the terms 'naturalism' and 'non-naturalism' for the two types of solution. So long as we are still considering the third view as a possible solution, however, the other terminology is to be preferred.

Moral principles, according to Hobbes, are rules about how to gratify our desires, and our desires have, ultimately, a biological origin. It follows that, if human nature were different, moral principles would be different. Moral principles, according to the moral sense school, are rules about how to gratify a special kind of desire or approval, which is quite apart from self-interest, but is an equally fundamental part of human nature. On this view, too, it follows that, if human nature were different, moral principles would be different.

But, it is objected, this is simply false. Take an assertion like 'cruelty is wrong'. The truth of this is not in the least dependent on your feelings or on mine. Suppose that there is a nation of sadists somewhere who feel no revulsion against cruelty, and so do not think it wrong; this does not in the least alter the fact that cruelty is wrong. Suppose that those sadists constituted the whole of the human race (as they well might in time,

51

4-2

as the result of natural selection) so that no one thought cruelty wrong; or suppose that human beings always had been sadists, so that no one had ever thought cruelty wrong; it would still be true that cruelty is wrong, always has been, and always will be, whatever human beings happen to think about it. Of course, nobody could know this fact, in the circumstances we are supposing, but it would none the less be a fact. In the days when everyone thought that the earth was flat, it was none the less round: just as round as it is now. In exactly the same way, intuitionists and rationalists claim, there are moral facts; and, as a consequence, moral statements whose truth or falsity does not depend on human beliefs or feelings.

This view should not, however, be misunderstood. There is a sense in which the truth of a statement like 'cruelty is wrong' obviously does depend on human feelings. If we ask why cruelty is wrong, part of the answer is that it is because human beings (and, of course, animals) feel pain. In a world in which nobody felt pain, there would be no need to make a rule against cruelty. But it is not true, even in this situation, that cruelty would not be wrong. What is true is that it would not be possible, in this situation, to be cruel. If cruelty (the wanton infliction of pain) were possible, it would still be wrong.

As things are, of course, men do feel pain. But they are not all pained by the same things. One man's treat is another man's torture. 'Oh,' cries the young man in Shaw's *The Music Cure*, 'don't, Don't, DON'T play classical music to me. Say you won't. Please.' Whether a particular action does cause pain or not may vary from individual to individual and so does depend, in a sense, on human feelings. But the generalization 'the wanton infliction of pain is wrong' does not depend on human feelings. This is just what the naturalist denies. According to Hutcheson and the other members of the moral sense school, for example, cruelty is wrong *because* it is repugnant to the moral sense: that is to say, because it runs counter to a particular human instinct or feeling.

On this view, then, the naturalist analysis of moral terms

must be rejected. '*X* is good' cannot be equivalent to '*X* has certain natural characteristics which evoke feelings of approval (in me or most men)' because feelings of approval (my own or anybody's) are quite irrelevant to its goodness. Since it seems clear that 'good' does not refer to any natural characteristic, anything that can be seen, touched, heard, smelt or tasted, we must conclude that it refers to a non-natural, or non-empirical, characteristic. We do not become aware of these characteristics through the senses, but we are aware of them none the less. Moreover, we are immediately, or directly, aware of them, just as we are aware of sensible qualities.

How do you know that your companion in the railway carriage is a middle-aged man? Well, his hair is grey, his face is lined, and so on. You know directly or immediately that he has these characteristics; from them you infer that he has the further characteristic of being middle-aged: that you know mediately, or indirectly. No one is likely to question that there are some things we know immediately. Must we suppose that immediate knowledge can be acquired only through the senses? If we are prepared to entertain the possibility that there are other ways of gaining immediate knowledge, the meaning of moral terms becomes less puzzling.

'*X* acted wrongly' is not an inference from (say) '*X* hit *Y* just because he enjoys causing pain', in the way that 'he is middle-aged' is an inference from 'his hair is grey'. We do not need to collect statistics of the number of actions of this kind that are wrong, as we might collect statistics of the number of grey-haired men who are middle-aged. Yet 'wrong' does not *mean* 'done from the motive of causing pain'. The wrongness of the action is a further characteristic, just as being middle-aged is a further characteristic of most grey-haired men. Once we know what the motive of the action is, we know immediately that it has the further characteristic of wrongness. We are aware of the wrongness of such a motive just as we are aware of the greyness of hair: immediately or directly.

The non-naturalist's name for such direct knowledge, when

it is not given through the senses, is 'intuition'. In many ways the term is an unfortunate one, suggesting some kind of second sight not possessed by ordinary men. Some critics have pointed out that the mathematical prodigy, who can tell you at once, without pausing for thought, the result of (say) multiplying 2,472 by 7,989, is often said to know the correct answer 'intuitively'. They have supposed that the intuitionist regards moral knowledge as being like this, and have protested that it is not. The prodigy knows, apparently without having to calculate, what the rest of us can discover by a process of calculation. But there is no process by which we can check the correctness of the claim that cruelty is wrong. The term 'intuition', these critics conclude, is a misnomer. We cannot doubt that the prodigy knows the right answer, because we can check it; but the ethical intuitionist is making a claim to knowledge which cannot be checked. He cannot point to any checking procedure which would enable us to test his claim. We need not, then, concede that such knowledge exists at all.

This is, however, to attribute to the intuitionist an argument which he does not use. 'Intuition' is, for him, a technical term used in a special sense, so that any appeal to the use of the term in 'ordinary language' is out of place. What the intuitionist says is simply that we know some facts directly, without inference or calculation: for example, that the grass we are now looking at is green. Most people will concede this so long as the knowledge is of sensible qualities. The intuitionist's contention is that some other qualities (or relations) are also known directly, and that moral characteristics are among them. This is, admittedly, a hypothesis: the intuitionist's argument for it is that it explains the facts as no alternative hypothesis can.

The intuitionist would not regard the achievement of the calculating boy as intuition in his sense at all. The paradigm cases he does put forward are quite different. There are, he argues, a good many facts which everyone knows without inference and which cannot be checked by the evidence of the senses but which no one seriously doubts: for example, that

$2 + 2 = 4$, that two straight lines cannot enclose a space, that a thing cannot be in two places at once, that nothing is both A and not-A at the same time, that if p implies q and q implies r, then p implies r. All these propositions, and many more, are, he claims, self-evident. It is hard to see how they could be proved, if anyone disputed them. We do not prove them, as we prove that this blade of grass is green, by looking and seeing. We can of course look and see that this particular pair of straight lines does not enclose a space; but our assertion goes beyond that. It also goes beyond saying that, in our experience, no two straight lines have ever been found to enclose a space, as we might say that no unstriped tigers have ever been discovered. For we are quite sure that no two straight lines *could* enclose a space, not as a matter of observed fact, but as something that, as we say, 'stands to reason'.

What is involved here is a controversy that goes beyond ethics. Or perhaps two controversies: the epistemological one about whether we can have knowledge of the world that does not rest on the evidence of the senses, and the metaphysical one about whether there are necessary facts, known by reason. For the propositions that the rationalist cites are not merely, he claims, as much statements of fact as any empirical propositions: they also have the great advantage of being indubitable. Unstriped tigers may turn up somewhere, just as black swans and egg-laying mammals turned up in Australia; but we can be quite sure that an instance of two straight lines enclosing a space will not be found even by the farthest-flung explorers in inter-stellar space. Reason, it is claimed, does not, like the senses, merely tell us what is the case, as a matter of fact: it tells us what must be the case, what cannot but be the case. There are, in short, two kinds of fact: penny plain or contingent facts, revealed to us through the senses, and twopence coloured or necessary facts, known through reason. Contingent facts are so called because they are contingent on the world being as it is, the laws of nature being as they are. Tigers are, as a matter of fact, striped, but they might easily have been unstriped. Necessary facts are not dependent on the way the world happens to be: it is inconceivable that two straight lines should ever enclose a space, or two and two make five, in this or any other planet.

The empiricist denies that there are any necessary facts. Facts are just facts: things are as they are, the world is as it is; we can find out just what they are, and how it is, only by the painstaking method of careful observation. Reason is very necessary, if we are to draw the right inferences from what we observe; but it does not provide a short cut by which we can discover what *must* be the case, regardless of observation. It does not, the empiricist argues, make sense to say that something must be the case, in the rationalist's sense. In ordinary speech we do of course say, for example, that if a man is deprived of oxygen he must die; but this is just an emphatic way of saying that men who have no oxygen to breathe do die, the laws of physiology being what they are. The rationalist claim that necessity is somehow an ingredient of some facts but not of others is, according to the empiricist, simply false.

As for the superior certainty, the indubitability, of those propositions alleged by the rationalist to state necessary facts, the empiricist may say, with John Stuart Mill, that these are ordinary empirical propositions of a very general kind. Their generality means that they have been exemplified so often in experience that it has become psychologically impossible for us to doubt them. More commonly nowadays, he will say that these propositions are actually analytic, and so tell us nothing about the world, but only about our use of words. Just as mermaids are necessarily fish-tailed, whether there are any mermaids or not, so two and two make four because of the definitions of those numbers, a thing cannot be in two places at once because (by definition) it would then be two things, and two straight lines cannot enclose a space (though this may not be apparent at first sight) because of the meanings of 'straight' and 'enclose a space'.

Any further discussion of the controversy between rationalists and empiricists would take us too far afield. It is clear, however, that the empiricist must take a naturalist position when he comes to consider moral philosophy. If nothing is in the mind that was not first in the senses, moral concepts, which are certainly in the mind, must refer to the kind of thing that can be experienced. '*X* is good', then, must be reducible without remainder to statements about the natural, or sensible, qualities of things and about our own desires, feelings of approval and the like. The naturalist analysis of moral terms is an attempt to make just this reduction.

Since the rationalist does not deny that *some* statements are empirical and *some* facts contingent, he could, without inconsistency, support a naturalist ethic. But, if there are any non-empirical facts, it seems very likely that moral propositions are among their number. Most of the problems that puzzle moral philosophers disappear if we are prepared to admit that there may be qualities or relations which are non-empirical. Moreover, moral propositions such as 'enjoying the pain of others is wrong', though not analytic, do seem to be necessary: it is hard to see how this could be right (as distinct from being thought right) in this or any other universe. Rationalists, then, have usually said that the ultimate premises of moral reasoning are synthetic necessary propositions expressing non-empirical facts known through reason and not through observation. It is this position that is meant when the term 'rationalism' is used in the context of moral philosophy.

Rationalists in ethics are, then, non-naturalists; but not all non-naturalists are rationalists. Some philosophers who reject the naturalist analysis of moral terms do so simply because they regard it as inadequate, without necessarily wishing to adopt the rationalist metaphysic. They do commit themselves to a belief in non-empirical qualities or relations, but not necessarily to a belief in synthetic necessary propositions, or in necessary facts. G. E. Moore, for example, insists that the naturalist analysis will not do, because '*X* is good' simply does not mean '*X* has certain natural qualities which rouse feelings of approval in me'. No such analysis, he contends, gives an adequate account of the concept of 'good' that we actually have. His conclusion is that 'good' refers to a 'simple quality' which cannot be further defined, but of which we are immediately aware. In this it is like 'yellow', but good differs from yellow in being non-natural, or non-empirical: that is, it is not known through the senses. In saying that 'good' is like 'yellow', Moore may be differing from those other intuitionists who say that 'X is good' is like '2 + 2 = 4'. It is not clear whether Moore would or would not say that good is known through the reason. He does say that good is not merely objective, but 'intrinsic', and the distinction he has in mind seems to be at least very like the rationalist distinction between the necessary and the contingent. He also says that the link between the goodness of X and those characteristics that make X good is a necessary, and not a contingent, one. Nevertheless, his main contentions about 'good' do not depend on a belief in necessary facts, and it would certainly be possible to adopt a position like Moore's without asserting that there are necessary facts.

In the broad sense of the term an intuitionist is anyone who believes that moral facts are known immediately, but not through the senses. A rationalist accepts this and also believes that this immediate knowledge is gained through reason, and that it is knowledge of something necessary and not contingent. (Reason, it is claimed, can give us immediate knowledge: the 'laws of thought', for example, are not inferences.) Since the intuitionist accepts part of the rationalist position, though not necessarily the whole of it, all rationalists are intuitionists, though some intuitionists may not be rationalists.

CHAPTER 6

MORAL PRINCIPLES AS POSTULATES

Since naturalists refuse to accept any basic unverifiable propositions except those recording the evidence of the senses, they
need to assimilate moral axioms to this type of proposition. As
we have seen, they do this by saying that the apparent difference
between the basic propositions of empirical reasoning and the
basic propositions of moral reasoning is not a real difference,
that, when properly analysed, moral axioms will be found to
record something that can be verified empirically, namely the
desires or attitudes of the person asserting them. Non-naturalists
on the other hand have argued that there are other basic propositions besides those recording the evidence of the senses.
Moral propositions, they say, state a particular kind of non-
empirical fact known by the reason rather than through the
senses, which is no worse a fact than those revealed by the
senses. But, as has already been mentioned, there is a third view
which has been put forward comparatively recently and which
it is claimed enables us to see that this traditional controversy is
a mistaken one.

This third view is briefly that moral principles are postulates
and not facts of any kind, whether empirical or non-empirical.
Its proponents point out that it is a mistake to suppose that even
reasoning about matters of fact need take only one kind of basic
proposition for granted, namely those which record the evidence of the senses. There are many other kinds of basic proposition, it is argued, which are equally indispensable. For
example, reasoning, whether about matters of fact or about
anything else, also takes for granted the principles of inference
according to which we are able to say that one proposition
follows from another proposition. Lewis Carroll's tortoise
demonstrated this point to Achilles in 1895. If the reasoning is
inductive rather than deductive a similar point can of course be

made, even more obviously perhaps, about the principles of induction. Scientific experiments, for example, proceed on the assumption that what has been found true of this or that sample of a given substance will be true of any sample of the same substance, provided that the conditions are the same. How can this assumption be proved? It may be said that it has worked in the past; but, if we infer from this that it will continue to work in the future, we are obviously assuming the very principle we are trying to prove. We assume this principle whenever we argue from cases we have observed to similar cases we have not observed. Since any argument from observation assumes this principle, it is clear that the principle itself cannot be observed to be true. The inductive principle, like the principles of deduction, must, it seems, simply be accepted without proof, for in the nature of the case no proof is possible.

Nor is this all. Empiricists claim that reasoning about matters of fact proceeds by means of inference rules, either deductive or inductive, from first premises which merely record what has been observed. But is it true that any statement *merely* records what has been observed? Thorough-going empiricists who have tried to formulate such statements have been reduced to staccato ejaculations like: 'This here now!' In order to assign a common name to what is observed here and now, it is necessary to make all kinds of implicit assumptions. Certainly one must presuppose the most general principles of logic, such as that A is A, that everything is either A or not-A, that nothing is both A and not-A. Probably one also needs such axioms as that a thing cannot be in two places at once. For to assign a common name (as distinct from a proper name) to something is to classify it, and classification is not possible unless we make such assumptions as these.

Many of the allegedly synthetic necessary propositions cited by the rationalist are in reality, some philosophers contend, very general rules of language built into the meaning of all the terms we use. Consequently the simplest statements, including those which we usually regard as merely recording observations, presuppose them. Since any statement presupposes them, they cannot be proved; for the proposition advanced as proof would be found to involve the same assumption, and the argument would be circular.

What now becomes of the sharp distinction between moral reasoning and empirical reasoning? It seems that they are, after all, in the same boat, or at least in very similar ones. It is true that moral reasoning begins with premises that cannot be verified, and must just be taken for granted. But so does empirical reasoning. The major premises from which it starts, the statements which record what we observe, themselves rest on further premises which cannot be supported by the evidence of the senses, and which there is no way of proving. Both empirical and moral reasoning, moreover, can proceed only by adopting rules of inference which are also unproven and unprovable.

Many of the points in the argument outlined above have been made in the past by rationalists. They, too, are fond of comparing fundamental moral judgements with the rules of inference; they, too, point out that neither can be proved, and add that neither need to be; they, too, claim that statements of this kind play a much larger part in empirical judgements than empiricists are willing to admit. But they regard all such statements as self-evident truths about the world. Consequently, they argue, we need not feel scandalized at regarding moral statements as also self-evident truths about the world, known with complete certainty, but incapable of proof and unsupported by the evidence of the senses.

The philosophers we are considering take a different view. In this they follow the lead of the mathematicians, who are no longer happy to accept mathematical axioms (such as 'two straight lines cannot enclose a space') as self-evident truths about the actual nature of space. A prevalent modern view is that they are postulates: that is to say, propositions asserted within the system but not necessarily holding outside it. To use a very popular analogy, postulates are, as it were, the rules of the game. When you play chess, the pawns move one square at a time in one direction only, and the queen as many squares as you like in any direction. You could play the game differently, but if you did it would not be chess. It might or might not be as good a game: that is, it might or might not amuse you, relax you and exercise your wits as efficiently as chess. Similarly, it is claimed, Euclid's axioms are, as it were, the rules of Euclidean geometry. You may, if you like, try to construct a geometry with different rules. In that case it would be a non-Euclidean geometry; it might or might not be as efficient in attaining the purposes for which one uses geometry.

Just as there are alternative geometries (Euclidean and non-Euclidean) so there are alternative logics (Aristotelian and non-Aristotelian). We may, if we like, construct a logic in which truth and falsity are not the only values: that is, in which the axiom 'If p is not true, then p is false' would not hold.

The ultimate premises, then, to which we appeal in any type of reasoning, whether mathematical, logical (in the formal sense), empirical or moral, are not self-evident truths about the world: they are axioms, or postulates, of the system that we happen to be using. They are essentially rules of procedure. To try to prove them is to mistake their status. They are the rules to which we appeal in order to prove other propositions within the same system. Hence they cannot themselves be proved. But it is equally a mistake to regard them as revelations about the nature of the universe, known by intuition.

These considerations, it is claimed, enable us to solve the whole problem about which naturalists and intuitionists dispute. The problem is solved by being dissolved: it is shown to be a pseudo-problem, based on a mistake. Once we realize that it is, in the nature of the case, impossible to prove any ultimate premises, we can see that there is no special problem about morals. Moral reasoning is no different from empirical reasoning in that respect. But that does not mean that the naturalist is justified in trying to reduce moral propositions to empirical ones. Moral postulates are different from the postulates of empirical reasoning, just as the axioms of geometry are not necessarily those of arithmetic. As it is often put, each system 'has its own logic'.

The proper course is to analyse carefully the principles to which we actually appeal in argument and reasoning, whether the reasoning is about morals or anything else. In this way we may discover what our postulates actually are. Having discovered them, and having discovered the rules of inference peculiar to moral discourse (for example, that it is legitimate to move from '*X* is right' to '*X* is what you ought to do'), we have completed our task. The further questions traditionally raised are pseudo-questions. They have never been satisfactorily answered because they do not permit of an answer. There is no point in trying to prove the postulates: to try to prove them is to show ignorance of what postulates are and of how they function within a system. There is no point, either, in manufacturing myths about 'intuition' as the special form of knowledge by means of which postulates are known, or about 'non-natural qualities' as the special kind of entity it knows. Postulates are not facts to be known, but rules of procedure to be adopted.

It is clear that, if this view is the right one, the controversy between naturalism and non-naturalism, with which many of the following chapters deal, is an idle one. So far we have been concerned with exposition of the opposing views rather than criticism. But it may be as well at this point to consider some reasons why the central problems cannot be dismissed quite as easily as the proponents of this view believe.

There are two possible lines of attack. One is to reject the whole thesis about postulates; the other is merely to deny that it applies to ethics. The second, or milder, criticism will be made first.

Let us grant, for the sake of argument, that in any system some propositions cannot be proved, since it is by reference to them that other propositions are proved. Does it follow that any postulate is as good as any other? Is it as rational to trust to the evidence of a sacred book, for example, as to the evidence of the senses? And what is to count as a system? Some philosophers have said that religious discourse is a system, or language, of its own and that it is a mistake to question such basic postulates of the system as that there is a God. Is there no limit to the multiplication of such systems, with their attendant unquestionable postulates? Is astrology or alchemy such a system?

The answer to this would be that a system is to be judged by its coherence, its complexity, and its elegance. The object of a mathematical or logical system, for example, is to begin with a very few postulates, undefined terms and procedural rules, and to deduce from these few elements a very large number of propositions or theorems. Considered in this light, Euclidean geometry is highly successful, even though it may need a little extra formalization to meet the strict requirements of a postulate set; so are the formal systems of logic developed in recent years. The only test that need be applied to any alternative system is whether it can, with equal ease and elegance, give rise to as large and varied a set of propositions.

Such a system must, however, be completely self-contained. If it relies on terms and concepts drawn from some other system, it is clearly incorporating that other system, and must be consistent with it if it is not to be guilty of incoherence. For example, if 'God exists' is interpreted as 'The universe was created and is sustained by an intelligent being', it is clear that religious discourse is taking over concepts from everyday speech and from science. This is, indeed, a cosmological hypothesis, and needs to be consistent with the scientific systems relevant to cosmology. 'God exists' can be regarded as a postulate immune from criticism only if 'God' is used in a special sense as a technical term within the system. Its use must not have any implications that would conflict with the conclusions reached within the system of empirical investigation. To claim, then, that religious discourse constitutes a system of its own with its own concepts and rules of procedure is to concede that, whatever its effect may be on the emotions of those who take part in this discourse, it has no relevance to our understanding of the way the actual world behaves. The most zealous atheist need not mind granting this much to religion, since it is really very little: far less, one imagines, than would satisfy most believers. Certainly astrologers and alchemists would not be satisfied with a like concession, since they do claim that their systems enable them to make predictions about the actual world. They are, then, setting up systems in competition with that of science, and may fairly be challenged to show that they are equally coherent and capable of accommodating as many elements.

Can a morality be fairly regarded as a system in this sense? It may be claimed that ethics does not compete with empirical systems, since ought-statements and is-statements are logically independent. It is true that moral reasoning usually contains both moral and empirical propositions. For example, suppose it is argued that slavery was justified in Greece because it made culture possible. Whether slavery did in fact promote culture is a question of fact. The moral proposition, 'whatever promotes culture is justified', is however quite independent of facts. It is sometimes said that a particular morality is based on superstition and delusion, but this applies only to the empirical minor premises, not to the moral major premises. A primitive tribe which believes that it is wicked to allow a woman to see an unfinished canoe because this will anger the spirits, who will show their displeasure by making the vessel unseaworthy, is no doubt deluded about the facts, but not about the prescriptive principle that whatever causes drowning is to be avoided.

It appears, then, that a moral system cannot be judged by its coherence with facts, as interpreted by any empirical system. How, then, is it to be judged? Presumably, by its internal coherence and its complexity. Let us suppose, for example, that the tribe were to adopt the opposite prescriptive principle: that whatever causes drowning is to be sought. If the system of which this principle is a part is not to be incoherent, presumably death in other forms will also be sought. But the injunction to seek death, if it is followed successfully, makes all other prescriptions unnecessary. The moral system of this tribe, then, is not capable of much complexity: it will consist in a very few, very exiguous principles.

But why, exactly, is complexity to be desired? If we make complexity the criterion by which moral systems are to be judged, are not we in fact implicitly assuming, as an over-riding value judgement, that a variety of activities and experiences is to be preferred to monotony, or to the complete cessation of all activity? Why should a system which does not itself include this prescription be expected to conform to it?

More generally, since the function of any value system is to lay down evaluative criteria, it may be doubted whether a moral system can be judged by such criteria. If we accept this there would seem to be one important difference between moral systems and the postulate sets that they have been compared with. It is true that this would not prevent a moral system from being a postulate set. It would merely mean that it is one of a peculiarly anarchic kind, not subject to the usual rules. Putting the point in another way, it may be argued that a system is in fact judged by its efficiency for the purposes for which it is used. An empirical system, for example, enables us to predict what will happen and will be discarded if, as a result of using it, our predictions are consistently unsuccessful. It may then be objected that since moral and other prescriptive systems are concerned to choose between purposes, this criterion cannot apply to them. This difference may well be connected with another one. If the principles of induction really do represent the minimal conditions of empirical investigation then we need not be surprised to find that talk of alternative principles of induction is purely academic, a philosopher's speculation rather than anything that is advanced very seriously. Similarly, if the laws of thought are the minimal conditions of intelligible discourse, we need not be surprised to find that in fact nobody does very seriously advance an alternative set. Talk of alternative logics, too, is a little misleading: the limits within which variations are seriously contemplated, not just talked about by philosophers, are really fairly narrow. Talk of alternative moralities on the other hand is not nearly so academic. It may be objected that most societies do have pretty much the same basic rules against, for example, killing, stealing, and so on. But although this is true it is also true, not only that there may be an extraordinary range of permissible violations of these principles in different societies, but also that one can, not uncommonly, come up, even in our own civilization, against a person whose basic moral principles seem to be fundamentally different from one's own. The logician on the other hand is not in real life confronted by Carroll's tortoise nor the scientist by someone who genuinely doubts the inductive principle.

The milder criticism then, which raises the question whether a moral system is in fact a postulate set, amounts to this. There are at least two points of difference which may very well be significant. First, a postulate set is in fact developed for a particular purpose and that purpose will dictate the criteria by which it is to be evaluated. A moral system, on the other hand, being a value system, is not susceptible of such criteria, for the existence of such criteria would imply the existence of a higher-order value system. We judge a system by whether it works or not, but it is far from clear what working would mean when applied to morality. It would normally be said that we cannot judge a morality, for example, by whether it causes us happiness or not. This is a prudential criterion, not a moral one. It is indeed the job of a moral system to say what it is that we shall regard as working or not working. For example, if a particular moral system bids us all to mortify the flesh to the point of seeking an early grave, and if as the result of the application of such a system the race speedily dies out, it cannot be said that the system has not worked: from its own point of view it has worked admirably. Nor could we even say that it had been proved wrong if nobody in fact had obeyed its precepts, so that the race did not die out. This would merely prove that humanity is frail and imperfect, incapable of living up to its ideals; it need not lead us to condemn the ideals themselves. Secondly, we do actually find ourselves confronted with alternative systems of morality whereas we do not, fortunately, often meet someone who tries to predict the behaviour of physical objects by postulating that nature is never uniform, or who refuses to accept the law of non-contradiction.

These points of difference between moral systems and the paradigm cases of postulate sets do not in themselves prove that a moral system is not a postulate set. But the point of making the comparison is to support the thesis that it is a mistake to try to justify, or call into question, the basic premises of moral reasoning, since these are postulates: that is, conventions which have no justification other than the system itself. Now what I am suggesting is that this is a mistake even when it is asserted about such postulate sets as arithmetic, logic or science. For, I am suggesting, while it is true in a sense that the postulates adopted in these disciplines are conventions, it is also true that the particular conventions adopted are those that are found to serve the purposes for which the system as a whole is adopted. For example, the logical postulates can be justified as what have been found to be the minimal conditions of intelligible discourse. The postulates of science (the inductive principle, for example) can be justified as what have been found to be the minimal conditions for understanding and predicting the behaviour of physical objects.

It is just this kind of characterization that is lacking for a moral system. What are the postulates of a moral system the minimal conditions of? Of living together in harmony with one another? But that presupposes the value judgement that one ought to live in harmony with others. And that would itself be a fundamental moral axiom being put forward, not as a postulate within the system, but as something outside the system by which the system is to be judged.

I think then that the differences (at least the first difference) that have been pointed out between moral systems and postulate sets do seriously affect the usefulness of the comparison.

Moral Principles as Postulates

We now come to the stronger criticism, which raises a further question: whether, assuming a morality to be a postulate set, it would follow that the traditional question at issue between naturalists and non-naturalists is a pseudo-question. What exactly, it may be asked, is being said by those who argue that a morality is, like a logical or mathematical system, a postulate set? There would seem to be three main possibilities:

1. They might be saying that mathematical, logical or empirical principles are to be taken for granted because, though they are not capable of proof, they cannot be doubted by any sane man, and must therefore simply be accepted as true. Moral principles, on this view, are to be accounted as equally certain and equally true.

2. They might be saying that mathematical, logical and empirical principles are simply, as it were, the spectacles through which we see the world. Others might conceivably don different spectacles. In that case they would see the world differently; but there would be no sense in which they would be wrong and we right.

3. They might be adopting a third view, which has just been adumbrated—that, while fundamental mathematical, logical and empirical principles are in a sense conventions, they are conventions adopted for a purpose. It is not true that any other conventions would serve the purpose equally well. Since the purpose is simply to understand the world, the conventions we use are in a sense forced on us by the way the world is.

Now the first of these views is pretty obviously just old-fashioned moral rationalism or intuitionism. It is, actually, ruled out by the view that a moral system is a postulate set, since we have been taking a postulate to be different from an assertion of fact, whether empirical or non-empirical. The second view is equally obviously old-fashioned subjectivism. The first two views about basic propositions, then, turn out to yield quite familiar traditional positions when they are applied to ethics. I want now to digress a little about the third view, although it is not strictly necessary to the argument to develop

69

it. Obviously it would be convenient to be able to say that, since this has been shown to be the right view about basic principles, we may accept the conclusions about moral principles that follow from it. It would, however, be outside the scope of this book to attempt a detailed defence of this third view. A little may nevertheless be said in support of it.

The view that the axioms of logic, etc., are postulates is not quite the same as the view that they are analytic propositions. But those who take this view probably would say that they are essentially rules of language, whose truth is guaranteed by definition. The difficulty one feels at first sight here is that one seems to be saying that basic propositions are purely arbitrary and conventional, that 'circles are never square' or 'nothing is both *A* and not-*A*' is like 'Foxes never have tails; they have brushes'.

One feels tempted to distinguish between these two, and to say that, if they are indeed both tautologies, one is a significant tautology and the other is a trivial one. This will no doubt seem odd and may need defending.

The first point is that, like nearly all analytic propositions, both significant and trivial tautologies depend on synthetic ones. For one, the relevant synthetic proposition is 'Some caudal appendages are attached to foxes, and some to other animals'. For another, it is 'Some figures are rectilinear, some curvilinear'. In each case we have an observed fact, which has been made the basis of a classification and so of a linguistic rule. So far, then, no difference.

But classifications may differ in at least two respects. Some may serve more purposes, or more central purposes, than others. The division of caudal appendages into brushes, which are attached only to foxes, and tails, which are attached only to other animals, may be useful to the fox-hunter, though even to him its usefulness is not very great. It would seem to be quite useless to anyone else. Or take another, very similar example: 'Men never sweat; they perspire.' Here again the division of animal exudations into perspiration, which exudes only from human bodies, and sweat, which exudes from other animals, would seem to be useful only for the purposes of the mealy-mouthed and ultra-refined. The distinction may well get in the way of other purposes, such as those of the physiologist.

This points to another difference between bases of classification. We expect a classification based on one characteristic to coincide in extension with a classification based on a different characteristic. We expect the distinction between tails and brushes or between sweat and perspiration to point to a difference in appearance or in chemical composition or at least in *something* apart from the animal of origin.

These two points of difference between bases of classification may be called respectively their *usefulness* and their *fruitfulness*. My suggestion is, then, that significant tautologies differ from trivial ones in that, while both express rules of language, the first are based on relatively useful and fruitful classifications, the second on relatively useless and fruitless ones. I say 'relatively', because this distinction is, of course, one that admits of degrees.

This may indicate how it is possible for a basic proposition to be analytic, a rule of language, and yet to be forced on us by the way the world is. The most basic propositions (for example, the laws of thought) may very well be the only ones, the world being as it is, that would serve the purposes for which we adopt them.

The usual argument against this is that these propositions cannot reflect the way the world is, since nothing would count as falsifying them. The answer to this is that, while it is true that our basic principles are made true by definition, it is also true that those definitions were framed in the first place because of the way that things are. It is quite true, certainly, that that one plus one equals two (for example) is not falsified by the fact that if you add one blob of mercury to another blob of mercury the result may be not two blobs of mercury, but one or seventy-five. But this is, after all, the exceptional case. Such an exception does not make us abandon the assertion that one plus one equals two. That remains true in the purely tautologous sense that it was one blob of mercury that was added to one blob of mercury in the first place, and that when you are able to say 'one plus one' you are also allowed to substitute 'two'. This becomes purely a verbal point. But the point is that if everything in the world behaved as blobs of mercury behave it is very unlikely that we would have adopted in the first place the arithmetical rules that we do in fact adopt. Or, to take another example, the causal principle: it is quite true, as has often been pointed out, that when we cannot find the cause of a particular event we do not regard this failure as falsifying the principle that every event has a cause. We simply assume that there is a cause, though we have not been able to discover it. Consequently, it is said, there is no possibility of falsifying the causal principle; it is the means by which we interpret events and no change in events would make us drop it. This, however, is probably just not true. It is quite possible that, if our efforts to find the causes of events failed much more often than they do, we would seriously consider abandoning the causal principle. Certainly the notion that a particular type of event might be outside the scope of the causal principle is not completely unintelligible to us. The revolutionary impact of Freud on the modern mind was partly due to his taking the causal principle quite seriously, as no one else was prepared to take it. He applied it, for example, to slips of the tongue. Common sense would no doubt concede that slips of the tongue do have a cause: some such cause as nervousness or haste. But this is not of course enough for Freud. He wants to know why the slip of the tongue takes the particular form it does, why we utter the particular syllable we utter. Here common sense is inclined to say that there is no answer to this question—that it is a matter of pure chance whether we utter the one syllable or the other. Freud is not prepared to accept this just because he pushes the causal principle to the limit: absolutely every event, including this one, must have a cause. The fact that many people still have sympathy with what I have called the common-sense view, as against Freud, suggests that we can at least conceive of the inapplicability of the causal principle to some types of event. And if to some, why not to others? Whether we accept Freud's explanation or not depends finally on how good a case he can make, on how well his hypotheses fit in with what we can observe. If they are not confirmed, we may well fall back on the view that the precise nature of a given slip of the tongue depends on chance. In the same way we accept the causal principle in other departments of life because the hypotheses to which it gives rise are, at least very often, confirmed by experience. If they were not confirmed, if our search for causes was unsuccessful very much more frequently than it is, we might very seriously consider abandoning the causal principle.

Well, these are some arguments, certainly not complete, in support of the third view of basic postulates. As I have said, this is something of a digression, because, whichever of the three views about basic postulates we apply to moral propositions, it will not follow that the traditional controversy has been proved otiose. The first view is simply intuitionism and the second view simply subjectivism. It is no doubt important that intuitionism and subjectivism apply to logic, mathematics and philosophy of science as well as ethics. But it is clear that, if one of these positions is being adopted, it cannot consistently be said that the question at issue between subjectivism and intuitionism in ethics is a pseudo-question, which disappears when the issues are seen clearly. The question is, on the contrary, one of the first importance, for other branches of philosophy besides ethics.

Nor does the third view offer any escape from this conclusion. The third view might lead to either of two positions, neither of them consistent with the view that the traditional problems of ethics are pseudo-problems. It might be used to support the conclusion that moral systems, since they do not have understanding the world as their purpose, are quite different from these other kinds of system. In that case, as has already been suggested, the parallel between moral systems and 'postulate

sets' breaks down. Alternatively, this third view might be used
to support a moral philosophy like that of Hobbes. Hobbes,
after all, would agree that any actual moral system is, in a sense,
a postulate set. Any actual society adopts certain moral principles, with which each new generation is indoctrinated; and to
say that an action is right is simply to say that it is consistent with
these principles. But the principles themselves are forced upon the
society by its purpose, which is to prevent a relapse into the anarchic state of nature; and this purpose is in turn forced on
the individuals who make up the society by their instinctive purpose, which is to gratify their desires. So interpreted, the third
view would lead to a naturalist ethic.

Actually, the philosophers who maintain that a morality is a
postulate set would protest against being forced to choose one
of these three views. Each of them, they would object, is a
metaphysical position: that is to say, it asserts something about
the nature of reality. Such assertions, they protest, are meaningless. So long as we confine ourselves to asking how we actually
reason about mathematics, or about the things we observe, or
about morals, we are on firm ground: we then discover that we
start from certain assumptions taken for granted. Once we
start to inquire about the ontological status of these assumptions
—how they are connected with reality, whether they state
non-empirical truths intuitively known, or are merely the
spectacles through which we see the world—we are asking
questions which, in the nature of the case, cannot be answered.
It is, indeed, even doubtful whether they can intelligibly be
asked, since it is hard to see what we are talking about when we
talk of 'reality' or of 'mental spectacles'.

To many philosophers, however, it will seem that, since we
do apply mathematical or logical or empirical assertions to the
world, these questions do in fact arise. No doubt they are hard
to answer; but we can at least try. If, as the result of trying, we
find ourselves talking nonsense, that is, after all, the occupa-
tional hazard to which philosophers are exposed. We should,
of course, guard against it as best we may; but to refuse to

answer these questions is not to dispose of them. The philosophers who do refuse to answer them, it may be said, are in fact implicitly assuming one or other of these positions (and sometimes sliding from one to the other and back again) without having the courage to admit it.

However that may be, it is at least clear that the analogy between moral axioms and these other kinds of postulate, even if it can be sustained, does not dispose finally of the questions at issue between naturalism and non-naturalism. Nor does it present a third view, which may enable us to avoid choosing between these two. Either the postulate set theory of ethics is a disguised form of subjectivism, or it is simply a refusal to consider the basic question at all, on the ground (insufficiently established) that it is a meaningless one. Those of us who are not convinced that it is meaningless and wish to discuss it may, then, confine ourselves to naturalism and non-naturalism as the only serious contenders in the field.

It has already been suggested that subjectivism is not an alternative either, since naturalism is bound up with subjectivism. Much the same may be said of the view that moral terms have emotive and not referential meaning, or that they are imperatives. Important points are made by these theories, but the points they make are not seriously at variance with naturalism. The naturalist theory, as I understand it, is that moral utterances express feelings of approval: in so doing, they prescribe ways of acting. To repeat, the naturalist analysis of 'X is good' is that it amounts to:

1. X has certain natural characteristics;
2. these characteristics are approved (by the speaker, or by most or all men).

Recent moral philosophers have done good service by pointing out that 'X is good' does not so much assert (1) as in some sense imply it, and that it does not so much assert (2) as express the feelings of approval to which (2) refers. It is also true that 'X is good' is not merely an expression of feeling, like 'Hurrah!'; it implies something about courses of action to be taken. But, although the traditional naturalists (Hobbes, Hutcheson, or Hume, for example) were not always as clear as they might have been on these points, there is no reason to believe that they would have disagreed with them. Nor do the philosophers who make these points seem, for the most part, to reject naturalism.

We shall, then, concentrate on naturalism and non-naturalism as still representing the two alternative answers to the central question of moral philosophy: the relation between fact and value. In doing so, we shall find that the questions discussed by recent moral philosophers still present themselves: for example, the 'universalizability' of moral principles, and the defining characteristics of 'moral' and related terms.

PART II

THE DEFENCE OF NATURALISM

CHAPTER 7

THE CASE AGAINST
NON-NATURALISM

From the lengthy war between naturalists and non-naturalists, two main arguments emerge on the naturalist side. The first of these may be called the metaphysical argument.

Most of us are prejudiced from the beginning against a theory which needs to invoke 'non-natural qualities'. And this prejudice may very well be justified. For what are these non-natural qualities which, according to the rationalist, we are more certain of than the world we see and touch, but whose existence we cannot demonstrate to the sceptic? Is not this just the kind of hocus-pocus that philosophers, of all people, should be most anxious to avoid?

It may be protested that this objection is based on nothing but dogmatism. Empiricists believe that there is nothing in the world except what can be known through the senses; but merely to assert this belief is no argument. The rationalist analysis of moral judgements is not to be dismissed out of hand simply because it does not conform to empiricist dogma.

It is not, however, dogmatic to insist that in this matter the onus of proof rests on the non-naturalist. Non-natural qualities may exist; but it is surely in order to call for evidence that they do exist. Merely to take their existence for granted would itself be dogmatism. The non-naturalist's case, then, rests on his assertion that the facts of morality cannot be satisfactorily explained without recourse to non-natural qualities. If the naturalist can produce an equally satisfactory explanation without resorting to them, then the advantage is on his side. The principle involved here is the one known as Occam's Razor: that entities should not be multiplied unnecessarily. If we need to invoke otherwise unknown entities in order to explain a phenomenon, this explanation is not to be accepted except as a last resort. We shall always prefer an explanation in terms of those entities of whose existence we have independent evidence. The non-natural ethical qualities that the intuitionist speaks of are clearly in this category: they are invoked for no other purpose but to explain the facts of morality. We should not adopt an explanation of this sort if there is an equally good explanation available which invokes only entities of which we have independent knowledge. If we accept the principle of Occam's Razor, then, the non-naturalist needs to show that the naturalist explanation is faulty, but it is not necessary for the naturalist to disprove non-naturalism. To say this is not just to assert empiricism dogmatically, unless, of course, the Occam's Razor principle itself is thought to be a piece of empiricist dogmatism.

The Occam's Razor argument may be made more specific. Non-naturalists do not of course deny that those things which have, according to them, the non-natural characteristic of goodness also have natural characteristics. Moreover, they agree that the moral characteristics of the thing arise out of these natural characteristics. They will say, for example, that it is because this action shows disinterested concern for others that it is a good action. Whenever we are told that something is good (or bad, for that matter) it always makes sense to ask: 'What is good about it? What other characteristics of the thing make it good?' It would be quite absurd to maintain that two things were exactly alike in all other respects but differed only in this, that one was good while the other was bad.

The non-naturalist admits, then, that moral characteristics are, to use Sir David Ross's term, 'consequential', or, to use Hare's term, 'supervenient'. Moreover, the non-naturalist admits that the perception of moral qualities will necessarily rouse certain feelings in men. He will say, for example, that we needs must love the highest when we see it or that we cannot help approving of what is good and disapproving of what is bad.

We have, then, this position: According to the non-naturalist

1. natural qualities give rise to
2. the non-natural quality of goodness which gives rise to
3. feelings of approval in human beings.

Now, the naturalist will ask, is the middle step here really necessary? Why not just say that the natural qualities of things produce feelings of approval in human beings and that we use moral terms in order to express these feelings? This would give us an explanation of the facts of morality without invoking any dubious entities.

The non-naturalist will reply, of course, that this explanation does not account for all the facts. For example, he will say that we cannot account for all the facts about moral judgements so long as we regard them as merely expressing our own likes and dislikes. What this amounts to is that the naturalist needs to supplement the metaphysical argument by his reply to the objections brought against naturalism. The metaphysical argument, then, is not conclusive by itself. It does, however, establish that the presumption is in favour of naturalism.

The second main argument against non-naturalism may be called the logico-psychological argument. Let us suppose with the intuitionists that 'good' is the name of a quality. To say that something is good is to make a purely descriptive statement like 'this buttercup is yellow'. There is no implied reference to feelings of approval. It follows from this, the naturalist argues, that to call something 'good' is to give no reason for pursuing it. The yellowness of buttercups is no reason for growing them or picking them unless you happen to like yellow. But we do think that to call something 'good' is to offer a reason for pursuing it, choosing it, bringing it into existence. It might of course be said that all human beings happen to be so constituted that whenever they perceive that something has this quality (goodness) they desire it or approve it. 'We needs must love the highest when we see it.' If the non-naturalist says this, however, he does seem to expose himself to the Occam's Razor argument given above. When we ask what exactly are the qualities that make us pursue or cherish something, or prefer certain courses of action to others, we do not point to some special quality of goodness or rightness but to the ordinary non-moral qualities: pleasantness, beauty, conduciveness to happiness, and so on. It seems hard to escape the conclusion that 'good' or 'right' are not the names of additional qualities but simply a way of indicating that we do approve or desire things which have these other, natural qualities.

It is clear that this argument depends on certain beliefs about what constitutes a reason for acting. It is bound up with what has already been said about means and ends. When asked to give a reason for our actions, we normally point out that the action in question is a means to a given end. If asked why we pursue that end we may point out that the end is itself a means to a further end. If asked to justify the end itself, however, we can only say, in effect: 'Well, that happens to be an end I pursue.'

This point is made quite forcefully by Francis Hutcheson. Suppose, he says, that we ask a man why he desires wealth. He may answer 'Wealth tends to procure pleasure and ease'. Again, suppose we ask him why he is prepared to risk his life in a just war. He may answer 'Such conduct tends to the happiness of my country'. Ask him why he serves his country, Hutcheson goes on, and he may say that his country is a very valuable part of mankind. In each case, Hutcheson concludes, the answer really consists in showing that the action is a means to an end: in the first case, the man's own happiness; in the second case, the happiness of mankind.

Hutcheson goes on to argue that it is impossible to advance a reason for choosing the end itself. He continues with the wealth example:

Ask his reason for desiring pleasure or happiness: one cannot imagine what proposition he would assign as his exciting reason. This proposition is indeed true; there is an instinct or desire fixed in his nature determining him to pursue his happiness; but it is not this reflection on his own nature, or this proposition, which excites or determines him, but the instinct itself. This is a truth 'rhubarb strengthens the stomach': but it is not a proposition which strengthens the stomach but the quality in that medicine. The effect is not produced by propositions showing the cause, but the cause itself.[1]

In other words, that the man instinctively pursues his own happiness is not a reason for his action but a cause. We desire happiness, but it is not reflection on that fact that makes us desire it. On the other hand, reflection on the fact that something is a means to happiness does make us desire it; we would not desire it unless we thought that it was a means to happiness. Hutcheson makes the same point about the other example. To realize that something is a means to the general happiness is a reason for pursuing it; but only because we already have a desire for the general happiness.

Hutcheson calls reasons of the means–end kind 'exciting reasons'. Exciting reasons, he says, presuppose affections: that is to say, desires. Hutcheson believes that in the last analysis there are just two basic affections, both of which are instinctive: self-love and benevolence. One need not, however, share this belief to accept his contention that what he calls exciting reasons presuppose desires which must just be taken for granted and cannot be further justified.

Exciting reasons are not, for Hutcheson, the only type of reason. He considers another example, a favourite one with eighteenth-century moralists. Let us suppose that a man strongly disapproves of luxurious living. We ask him why, and his answer is: 'Luxury evidences a selfish base temper.' Here it is not a question of a means to an end. The reason for avoiding luxury is simply that luxury is a certain kind of thing or that it springs from a certain kind of disposition. But this would not be a reason for avoiding luxury, Hutcheson maintains, unless we had certain feelings about things of that kind. The reason given amounts to saying that we dislike or disapprove of luxury. Hutcheson believes that feelings of disapproval are at bottom instinctive and common to all men. Ultimately, he thinks, we disapprove of any action which reveals that the agent has

---

[1] 'Illustrations upon the Moral Sense', Section 1. See *An Essay on the Nature and conduct of the Passions and Affections with Illustrations on the Moral Sense* (3rd ed. London, 1742), p. 221.

6-2

subordinated the instinct of benevolence to the other instinct of self-love. Again, however, we need not share this belief to accept his contention that reasons of this kind amount to asserting that we happen to have certain feelings of approval or disapproval. Hutcheson calls reasons of this kind 'justifying reasons'. Exciting and justifying reasons, he says, are the only kinds that there can be. Both consist ultimately in an appeal to human sentiments or attitudes: and it is not possible to justify those attitudes themselves.

Hutcheson makes his position quite clear in the course of his controversy with Balguy.[1] Balguy had asked Hutcheson whether God had any reason for endowing man with the kind of disposition that approves of kindness and disapproves of cruelty rather than one which approves of cruelty and disapproves of kindness. Obviously, if he had some reason, then there is some reason, quite apart from human dispositions, for preferring kindness to cruelty. Kindness really is better than cruelty in the eyes of God, that is, to a being who sees things as they are in themselves and not as coloured by the peculiarities of the human constitution. If God had no reason then, Balguy suggests, both man and God must be supposed to act merely from blind impulse.

Hutcheson, in his reply, makes two main points. First, he says, when we talk of an action done from blind impulse we usually mean one whose consequences are neither foreseen nor desired by the person acting. Moral dispositions are not 'blind' in this sense. But if by 'blind impulse' is meant a desire for which no further justification can be given, then there is no escape from blind impulse either for man or for God. The only reason that we can have for pursuing an end is that we happen to desire or approve it. The only reason that God can have for wishing us to pursue an end is that he happens to desire or approve it. The attempt to avoid 'blind impulse', in this sense, merely lands us in an infinite regress. 'God's willing to regard the fitness of

1 Richard Balguy, *Foundation of Moral Goodness* (London, 1728). Hutcheson's reply is in the 'Illustrations upon the Moral Sense', pp. 243 *et seq.* of the edition cited above.

things must be a blind impulse unless he has a prior reason why he wills what his understanding regards as fit, rather than as unfit; for his understanding represents both. And there must be a prior fitness that he should regard the fitness of willing what is fit, and so on.'[1]

Hutcheson drew one conclusion that was later made much of by Hume. The conclusion is that no end is more rational than any other. It is irrational to adopt something as a means if we have reason for believing that it will not in fact lead to the desired end. If I want to go to Adelaide from Melbourne it is clearly irrational to get on a train that I know is going to Sydney. Similarly, it is irrational to go to Adelaide for the sole purpose of doing something which could be done more easily and more efficiently somewhere nearer at hand. If, however, an end is pursued for its own sake, not as a means to a further end, then there would seem to be no criterion by which we can judge it to be irrational. As Hume puts it, in a famous aphorism: ''Tis not contrary to reason to prefer the destruction of the whole world to the scratching of my finger.'[2] Hume is here merely sharpening and dramatizing a point that had already been made by Hutcheson when he said:

Should anyone ask even concerning these two ultimate ends, private good and public, is not the latter more reasonable than the former? What means the word reasonable in this question?...If the meaning of the question be this, 'does not every spectator approve the pursuit of public good more than private?' the answer is obvious, that he does: but not for reason or truth, but from a moral sense in the constitution of the soul.[3]

The main point in all this is that no assertion that something is the case can, in itself, provide a reason for action. It follows that if moral statements do provide a reason for action they are not assertions that something is the case. This means that the standard non-naturalist analysis of moral statements is wrong. 'X is good' cannot mean merely that X has a particular non-natural quality.

[1] 'Illustrations upon the Moral Sense', *op. cit.* p. 243 n.
[2] *Treatise*, Book II, Part 3, Section 3.
[3] 'Illustrations upon the Moral Sense', *op. cit.* p. 229.

This argument has been put forward again in recent years by those who insist on the distinction between descriptive statements and other types of utterance. Much confusion may be avoided, it is contended, if we recognize that it is the function of many utterances not to describe or assert but, for example, to express emotions or to prescribe ways of acting. It is sometimes added that this contention throws a completely new light on moral philosophy. Traditional moral philosophers, it is suggested, ignored the distinction and treated all moral utterances as if they were assertions. It is very doubtful whether this charge can be fairly levelled against the traditional naturalists: for example against Hobbes, Hutcheson or Hume. It has always been central to the naturalist case that, since moral utterances provide reasons for acting and since the only reasons for acting are human attitudes, moral utterances must express human attitudes. Recent moral philosophers have done valuable work in elaborating the distinctions involved; but it is important to realize that in making these distinctions they are not putting forward a completely new position in moral philosophy, but are supporting the traditional naturalists in what has always been one of the main arguments against non-naturalism.

CHAPTER 8

THE NATURALISTIC FALLACY

Just as the naturalists have traditionally urged two main arguments against non-naturalism, so non-naturalists have traditionally urged two main arguments against naturalism. These will be stated in the next chapter. In this one I shall consider an argument put forward by G. E. Moore, which is often regarded as being quite conclusive against naturalism. I shall contend that it has force only against a position that has not been held by any actual naturalist. Indeed, one point it makes (perhaps obliquely) is more damaging to Moore's own position than to the views held by the naturalists he attacks.

Moore accuses the naturalist of committing a fallacy, which he christens 'the naturalistic fallacy'.

As we have seen, the naturalist solves the problem of verifying moral propositions by means of definition. If moral statements can be reduced without loss of meaning to statements about the sort of thing that can be observed (including our own desires and feelings of approval, which are observed by introspection), the epistemological problems about morality are solved. So is the logical problem about the transition from 'is' to 'ought'.

But, Moore argues, the naturalist can adopt this solution only if he is prepared to accept certain consequences. If he puts forward a definition, he must be prepared to treat it as a definition: that is to say, as an analytic statement and not a synthetic one. According to Moore, there is one sure test of an analytic proposition. If 'X is Y' is analytic, then the question 'Is Y X?' will not make sense. A moment's reflection will make us realize that to ask it is to ask 'Is X X?', a question that would certainly puzzle us. For example, we would be puzzled if anyone were to ask, in all seriousness, 'Is a father a male parent?' We would be at a loss to know just what he was doubting.

Now, Moore argues, any statement of the form 'good is X', where X is some natural object or characteristic, gives rise to a perfectly genuine and intelligible question. Hobbes, for example, defines 'good' as 'the object of desire'; but we may ask 'Is the object of a desire always good?' This is an intelligible question. Even if our answer is 'yes', we can quite well understand the grounds on which someone might answer 'no'. It follows that 'whatever is desired is good' is a synthetic statement. It is not, therefore, a definition.

Furthermore, Moore contends, the naturalist definitions are never treated by the naturalists themselves as if 'good is X' were equivalent to 'X is X'. Hedonists, for example, put forward 'good is pleasure' as a definition. But the hedonist also wants to use his definition as an argument: he wants to advocate the pursuit of pleasure, and the reason he gives is that pleasure is good. If he meant no more by this than that pleasure is pleasure, he would not be able to put this forward as an argument. Moore says that any naturalist will try to use his definition as an argument. It follows, then, on the naturalist's own showing, that his definition is not, by this test, a genuine definition.

The naturalistic fallacy has been discussed a good deal since Moore first drew attention to it. The accounts given of it do not always correspond with the one given above. Before proceeding further, then, it may be as well to say something about these other versions of it.

Some philosophers refer to the naturalistic fallacy as if it were identical with the failure to distinguish between prescriptive and descriptive language. Moral utterances, they point out, never simply describe: never simply say that X has such-and-such a characteristic, Y. They also have implications for conduct. To say that X ought to be done, or even that X is good, is not merely to describe X, but is, at least by implication, to urge the hearer to do something about X, if only to think well of it. Consequently any definition of moral terms that makes them purely descriptive is bound to be inadequate. That is why we feel that, in the naturalists' definitions, the *definiens* is never precisely equivalent to the *definiendum*: that something has been left out. What has been left out is the prescriptive element.

Now it may well be that this is why Moore is right when he says that any proposition of the form 'good is X' (where X is a natural characteristic) will never seem to us to mean the same as 'X is X'. But it is quite misleading, all the same, to regard the naturalistic fallacy as simply the same as confusing prescriptive with descriptive language.

Certainly Moore himself did not think of the naturalistic fallacy in this way. For Moore the typical moral proposition is 'X is good', and he regards this as an exact parallel to 'X is yellow': that is to say, as a descriptive statement. Moore's position rests on an epistemological atomism. The things we know can be analysed into simple qualities (or relations, presumably) that cannot themselves be analysed, but are known immediately. Sense perception is the paradigm case of immediate knowledge, and yellow is a paradigm case of a simple quality. But there are also non-natural qualities, which may also be known directly, though not through the senses. Good is a quality of this kind: a simple, non-natural quality. Consequently 'X is good' is like 'X is yellow', except that it cannot be empirically verified.

Moore seems to think of definition as the analysis of a complex into the simple qualities and relations of which it is made up. It follows that a simple quality is itself indefinable. Consequently Moore regards 'good' as indefinable. What we can do with a simple quality is to state its relation to other things. We can, for example, state the position of yellow in the spectrum, or the causal relation between yellow and light-waves of a particular wavelength. But these will be synthetic statements, not analytic ones. Consequently they can never be definitions.

Moore would not, I think, deny that we can define simple qualities in the sense of finding synonyms for them. There is no reason why one and the same simple quality should not happen to have two names. The word 'good' and the word 'desirable', for example, may very well be alternative names for the same simple quality. But, of course, no term which has as its referent a natural characteristic could also be the name of a non-natural characteristic. Synonymous naturalist definitions of 'good' are, accordingly, ruled out as well as analytic definitions, though for a different reason.

Moore's objection, then, is to treating as a definition a statement which, being synthetic, cannot be a definition. It is not to treating a prescriptive utterance as a descriptive one, for he does regard 'X is good' as descriptive. He is not concerned either with Hume's problem of the impossibility of deducing 'ought-statements' from 'is-statements'. Moore is quite prepared to say that 'X ought to exist' (or 'one ought to bring X into existence') follows from 'X is good'.

It is arguable, of course, that in the naturalistic fallacy Moore had stumbled upon something whose true nature he did not understand. But it is worth noticing that two paradoxical consequences follow from identifying the naturalistic fallacy with the confusion between prescriptive and descriptive language. One is that Moore himself is guilty of the fallacy; the other is that the traditional naturalists are not.

The traditional naturalists do not simply identify good with a natural characteristic. They rather say that moral terms contain an implicit reference to the fact that human beings in general have feelings of approval for the characteristic in question. This is, of course, quite clear in the moral sense school: the whole eighteenth-century controversy about whether feeling or reason is the basis of morality turns on this very point. It is equally clear in Hobbes and in those utilitarians, like Bentham, who take psychological hedonism as their starting-point. It is certainly arguable that this implicit reference to approval allows sufficiently for the prescriptive element in moral language.

A rather different account of the naturalistic fallacy is given by W. K. Frankena.[1] Frankena points out that Moore says in

---

[1] In *Mind* (1939; reprinted in W. Sellars and J. Hospers, *Readings in Ethical Theory*, New York: Appleton-Century-Crofts, 1952).

one place that to define pleasure as the sensation of red would be 'the same fallacy which I have called the naturalistic fallacy'. It appears from this that one commits the naturalistic fallacy whenever one identifies any characteristic, natural or non-natural, simple or complex, with a different characteristic. This is, according to Frankena, what the naturalistic fallacy really amounts to. Consequently he says that it might well be called the definist fallacy. To attempt to define the indefinable, in Moore's sense, is just a special case of this general fallacy, for it amounts to identifying a simple characteristic with a complex one. Similarly, to identify a non-natural characteristic with a natural one would be another special case of the same fallacy. A further special case is to identify an ethical characteristic with a non-ethical one. Ethical naturalists are guilty of all of these special forms of the fallacy at one and the same time because what they do is to identify a simple non-natural ethical characteristic with a complex natural non-ethical one. We have some temptation to commit the fallacy whenever we are confronted with a simple and so indefinable quality because we are reluctant to admit that any qualities are indefinable. Similarly, we are likely to commit the fallacy whenever we are confronted with a non-natural quality because we are also reluctant to believe that any qualities can be non-natural. It is hardly surprising, then, that moral philosophers should have made this mistake. No doubt in christening the fallacy Moore did have in mind, in particular, the confusion of non-natural characteristics with natural ones, but he himself recognizes that the fallacy is much wider in scope than the name would imply. It is a general kind of mistake which naturalists are especially prone to. If we ask just why this is a fallacy, what is fallacious about it, the answer is that it is wrong because it is identifying a characteristic with a different one.

But in that case, Frankena goes on, it is not properly speaking a fallacy at all: it is a material mistake, not a formal one. No one ever sets out to define one characteristic in terms of a different one. What he says is that the two terms are the names of one and the same characteristic: there are not two characteristics here, but one. There is nothing absurd in this contention in general: it is not absurd to say that two different words may be used to refer to the same characteristic: for example, that 'good' and 'pleasant' refer to the same characteristic. Any such claim needs to be investigated on its merits. It cannot be ruled out in advance as necessarily fallacious. The naturalist, then, according to Frankena, has not been convicted by Moore of any fallacy. He may be making a mistake, but it is up to Moore to show that he is making a mistake. The whole question at issue is whether ethical characteristics can, in fact, be identified with natural non-ethical ones. If they cannot, then of course it is a mistake, though not a fallacy, to say that they can be. But Moore is merely asserting against the naturalist that the naturalist view is a mistaken one: he has not done what he purports to do, namely, to show that any attempt to prove the naturalist position will involve the naturalist in a logical fallacy.

That is in outline Frankena's case against Moore, as I understand it. I think, however, that when we look at Moore's actual arguments, we may find that it is possible to defend him against Frankena's case.

Moore, as we have seen, has two main arguments. One is that it always makes sense to ask, of any natural object or characteristic, whether it is in fact good. The other is that no statement of the form 'X is good' (where X is a natural object or characteristic) is ever precisely equivalent to 'X is X'.

Each of these arguments may be generalized. We may say:

1. Anyone commits a fallacy who asserts, at one and the same time,

    (i) a proposition of the form $X = p, q, r$ (def.);

    (ii) that 'Is (p, q, r) X?' is an intelligible question.

2. Anyone commits a fallacy who asserts, at one and the same time,

    (i) a proposition of the form $X = Y$ (def.);

    (ii) that 'X is Y' asserts something different from 'X is X'.

According to Moore, naturalists will inevitably make the

first of these mistakes, and probably the second as well. Since good is in fact a simple non-natural quality, it will always make sense to ask, of any natural object or characteristic, whether it is good. Moreover, the naturalist, as we have seen, usually wants to use his definition as an argument for pursuing X (pleasure or evolutionary development or whatever it may be); and he cannot do this if 'X is good' means 'X is X'.

According to Frankena, the alleged fallacy, in its broadest form, is the identification of any characteristic with a different one; and this, he says, is not a fallacy. What I am suggesting is that the fallacy, in its broadest form, is treating a definition as a synthetic proposition. According to Moore, no proposition is analytic if it gives rise to an intelligible question, or if the subject and predicate are not clearly synonymous. Now I think that treating a synthetic proposition as if it were an analytic one has some claim to be called a formal fallacy. Consequently, I think that Frankena is wrong in saying that Moore has nothing more than simple assertion to urge against the naturalist. Moore does, of course, need to show that the naturalist is putting forward a proposition which he claims to be an analytic one, and is then treating it as if it were a synthetic proposition. But Moore does in fact have arguments, which are by no means negligible ones, to show that the naturalist actually does do this.

Nevertheless, I also think that the naturalist has quite adequate defences against Moore's arguments. The naturalist can reply to Moore's first argument by denying that definitions can never produce intelligible questions. Or, if Moore insists on using the word 'definition' so as to conform with this criterion, he may say that what he is putting forward is not a definition in that sense, but an analysis of moral concepts.

Suppose we take the example 'A father is a male parent'. At some stage in a child's life this will certainly convey genuine information; and it follows that at some stage in a child's life the question 'Is a father a male parent?' will be, for him, a genuine question. The child first learns the word 'father' by a process of ostensive definition. He knows that Dad is his father, that Mr Brown is Johnny's father, that Mr Smith is Jimmy's father, and so on. It may be some time before he discovers the characteristics which each of these relationships has in common. For a time he may make mistakes about this. He may, for example, refer to Mr Brown not only as Johnny's father, but also as Fido's father, because Fido is also a member of the Brown household. At this stage he mistakenly supposes that 'father' means 'head of the household' or, more accurately perhaps, 'senior male member of the household'. At a rather more sophisticated stage he may be puzzled when told that the person he has always supposed to be Bill's father is not his real father at all, but only a stepfather. In much the same way, it may be argued, the child gradually learns the meaning of terms like 'good' and 'right' by slowly discovering what there is in common in the various actions for which he is praised and rewarded by his parents and teachers. At any given moment he may be in doubt about whether his analysis is the correct one and accordingly any definition which he poses to himself may give rise in his mind to a perfectly genuine question of the form 'Is p, q, r good?' This need not prevent the definition from being, in fact, the right one.

It may be objected to this that in the 'father' case the child is in fact using the word 'father' to mean whatever there is in common in the relation that holds between himself and Dad, between Johnny and Johnny's father, between Jimmy and Jimmy's father, and so on. At this stage this would provide him with the only genuine definition of 'father': the assertion that a father is a male parent is at this stage a synthetic proposition. It is only when he goes on to apply the word 'father' to all other male parents that he may be said to be using 'a father is a male parent' as a definition; and when he has reached this stage the question 'Is a father a male parent?' will no longer be for him a genuine question. Similarly, it may be argued, 'good' or 'right' is being used to mean 'whatever there is in common in the various actions which my parents and teachers praise'. It is only when the child goes on to apply moral terms to actions which have not been praised by his parents and teachers, but which are of the same general kind, that he may be said to be using 'X is good' as a definition; and now this assertion will no longer give rise to a genuine question.

This is, however, to simplify the situation. A child, and an adult for that matter, need never explicitly formulate to himself those characteristics which the actions praised by his parents and teachers have in common. It is just that he forms habits of regulating his conduct as a result of his early training: he has been conditioned to approve of certain kinds of actions and to disapprove of others. When somebody points out to him what it is that these actions have in common, he may well be surprised. It may still be said, of course, that even in this case terms like 'good' and 'right' may be said to mean 'whatever criteria I do in fact use to regulate my conduct'. No naturalist, however, would be concerned to deny this.

The naturalist's first answer to Moore, then, is that a definition, or at least the analysis of a concept, may very well give rise to a quite genuine and so intelligible question. For example, the utilitarian may say that people use 'right' to mean 'conducive to the general happiness', but that they do not usually realize this. They have been conditioned to approve of actions which are, in fact, conducive to the general happiness, they regulate their conduct by this standard, but they need the utilitarian to point out to them exactly what the standard is. On reflection they may come to agree that this is, in fact, the standard they use; but since it takes a good deal of reflection to discover this, the question whether this is in fact the standard will be a perfectly intelligible one.

There is, however, a second argument that the naturalist may also use. He may say that his assertion is not so much that 'good' means X, in Moore's sense of 'means', as that 'good' *really* means X. The difference between 'means' and 'really means' may be brought out by an illustration. I find this definition of 'taboo' in a textbook of Social Psychology (it is meant as a definition because it comes from the glossary of terms at the back of the book): 'A taboo is a socially accepted prohibition of an act.' Now one might well imagine a native whose life was circumscribed by taboos protesting against this definition. A taboo act, he might say, is one forbidden by the spirits of our ancestors, one which will be punished by them, one from which all right-minded men recoil with instinctive horror, and so on. The social psychologist would, I imagine, reply: 'This is certainly part of the meaning of the word for you. I don't dispute that. But I stick to my definition because this seems to me all that there really is in the word, all that it has of cash value. I can't find your spirits or the punishment they are alleged to inflict. I can find a social attitude and the punishment imposed by society.' Now one could well argue that this alleged definition of taboo is not a true definition if by that we mean a statement of the connotation of the term, its meaning to the speaker. At the same time, it is not adequate to say that what the social psychologist really means is that whenever an act is forbidden by the spirits, etc., there is also a socially accepted prohibition of that act. He wants to say much more than that: he wants to say that the socially accepted prohibition is all that is substantial in the anger of the spirits. He wants, in fact, to prune away part of the connotation of the word as mistaken. In the same way the hedonist, for example, does not want to say, as Moore suggested, that whatever is good is also pleasant. What he wants to say is that, while people who use the word 'good' may very well have at the back of their mind some vague notion of a non-natural quality, there is no such non-natural quality in fact.

Take another parallel. The naturalist is, on this view, saying much the sort of thing that in another field is being said by the phenomenalist. The phenomenalist may well say that the meaning of any statement about physical objects is some other statement about sense data. One might easily use Moore's argument against him: one might ask, for example, whether the question 'is a table just such and such a set of sense data?'

is an intelligible question, one about which we need to ponder. I do not think, however, that anyone would regard this as an adequate refutation of phenomenalism. The phenomenalist, the social psychologist and the naturalist are all, in their different fields, debunking. And, of course, if their definitions fail to give rise to intelligible questions, there would be nothing to debunk.

If we have a look at what ethical naturalists actually say, I think we will find that they mean their definitions in this way. They do not mean to give the accepted connotation of the term 'good' or whatever; they do mean to debunk the accepted connotation, to reduce it to what alone is, they claim, of substantial value. Consider this naturalist definition: 'whatsoever is the object of any man's appetite, that is it which he for his part calleth Good; and the object of his hate and aversion, Evil'. Now as a definition this is certainly more than usually open to Moore's method of attack. It not only makes sense to ask 'Is the object of desire always good?' but it is very hard to see how the answer can be anything but 'No'. We commonly say that some desires are bad, and some people have said that desire as such is bad. But it is important to see what Hobbes is doing here. The definition falls into place as part of a theory of the passions. According to Hobbes, the passions are essentially minute movements in the body: 'the small beginnings of motion within the body of man'. When the motion is a reaching out towards something, we call it appetite; when it is a shrinking back from something, we call it aversion. This is simply what we observe in animals, when the kitten reaches out for the bird, or when the bird flutters away from the kitten. If they could speak, we might well imagine them saying 'good' and 'bad' respectively. What Hobbes is saying, in short, is that this is how the concepts 'good' and 'bad' arise. This is how they fit into the physical universe: this is their essential meaning. No doubt in man this simple reaching out for and shrinking back from has become modified by all sorts of associations of one kind and another. Obviously, to make his findings fit the facts, Hobbes has a good deal of explaining (and explaining away) to do. It is perfectly relevant to say to him that this is not the way we use the word 'good', that it makes sense to say that the objects of some desires are not good. To put forward this objection is to ask him to explain how his theory fits the facts. But it is not, I think, to the point to say simply that the question 'Is the object of desire always good?' is an intelligible one, or that 'good is the object of desire' means something different from 'good is good'.

I now want to say something about Moore's second argument. Consider again the naturalist who defines 'right' as 'conducive to the greatest happiness of the greatest number'. We object that we think it right to keep promises, even when they do not conduce to the general happiness. Now he may reply, as many naturalists have replied, that this is a mistake: that really we only think promise-keeping right because in the long run keeping promises always does conduce to the general happiness. But it is also possible that he may reply, if pressed, that, although we do think promise-keeping right, we are mistaken. It is not right at all, he may say, or at least not always right. Why is it not right? Because it does not always make for the general happiness. And some utilitarians have, of course, said this.

Now here Moore will say that, in the mouth of the utilitarian, 'promise-keeping is not right because it does not make for the general happiness' ought to mean no more than that promise-keeping does not make for the general happiness because it does not make for the general happiness, and this is, of course, no argument. What the naturalist has to say here is, I think, something like this: 'If you ask yourself what you really approve you will discover, if you are honest with yourself, that you approve of actions which make for the general happiness. Admittedly your first non-reflective tendency is to approve of keeping promises, even in those cases when they do not make for the general happiness. If, however, you carefully examine the implications of approving of such actions, I think you may be led to retract this approval.'

What this amounts to is that the naturalist analysis of 'X is right' or 'X is good' is that it is equivalent to (a) X has a given natural characteristic p; (b) p is approved (by me or by men in general). The utilitarian, for example, wants to say that men do in fact approve of actions which are conducive to the general happiness and that, in calling these actions right, they are referring both to the fact that they are conducive to the general happiness and to the fact that they are approved. It is a mistake to suppose that the traditional naturalists regarded moral terms as reducible without remainder to terms referring to objective characteristics. They did regard moral terms as reducible without remainder to terms referring to objective natural characteristics *and* to human feelings, in particular feelings of approval.

This is relevant to Moore's second argument. It is true that naturalists do commonly use their analyses as arguments. Now to say that an action has a particular characteristic (for example, that it is conducive to the general happiness) is not a reason for doing it, even if 'right' means 'conducive to the general happiness'. This is indeed, as we saw in the last chapter, one of the principal naturalist arguments against non-naturalists, like Moore. But that an action is the kind of action you approve is a reason for you to do it. Consequently naturalists are, after all, entitled to use their definitions as arguments. They are entitled to do so because of the second element in those definitions. Taken in this way, this argument tells more heavily against Moore himself than against his opponents.

CHAPTER 9

OTHER ARGUMENTS
AGAINST NATURALISM

The naturalistic fallacy has been treated separately because of the immense interest that it has aroused in recent years. Apart from it, however, there are two arguments which have been traditionally used by non-naturalists in attacking naturalism, and which do go to the roots of the uneasiness which most people feel when they encounter naturalism for the first time. We may call these the anti-relativist argument and the authority argument respectively.

Moore's attack on naturalism might be put in the form of a dilemma. Either, it might be said, the naturalist commits the naturalistic fallacy, or he is involved in relativism. If he says that 'good' just means 'pleasant' he is faced with the patent fact that 'good' has all sorts of implications that 'pleasant' does not have. If, on the other hand, he says, as I have suggested that he does, that 'good' means 'having certain natural characteristics which rouse feelings of approval in most men', then he must admit that 'good' and 'bad', 'right' and 'wrong', depend on human feelings and would be different if they were different.

That naturalism does imply relativism comes out quite clearly in the controversy between Hutcheson and Balguy already referred to. Hutcheson holds, it will be remembered, that to call something 'good' is just to say that it has those qualities which men do, as a matter of fact, approve of: that men approve of these characteristics is just a fact of human nature. Hutcheson's term for this human disposition to approve of some things and disapprove of others is, of course, 'the moral sense'. Balguy asks Hutcheson, very shrewdly, why God endowed us with the kind of moral sense we happen to have rather than with one which might make us, for example, approve of cruelty and disapprove of kindness. Was this, he asks, merely an arbitrary whim on God's part, or did God have some reason? Obviously if he had a reason then there is some reason, quite apart from the moral sense, for preferring kindness to cruelty. Kindness really is better than cruelty in the eyes of God; that is, in the eyes of a being who sees things as they are in themselves, and not merely as they appear to a human being with a particular kind of constitution. On the other hand, if God had no reason, then it was a mere matter of chance that men have the kind of moral sense they do have, and we cannot say that in any objective sense good is better than evil.

Hutcheson's reply is that God himself must be supposed to have something analogous to the moral sense. God, that is to say, did have a reason: namely that kindness was approved by his moral sense, and cruelty disapproved. No other kind of reason is possible, either for God or for man.

Balguy then asks whether the possession of a moral sense is a perfection in God or not. If it is not a perfection, it follows that a different God, who preferred cruelty to kindness, would be equally perfect. If it is a perfection in him, then this is another way of saying that kindness really is better than cruelty, quite apart from the moral sense. Hutcheson's reply is simply to reiterate that words like 'good' or 'better' can have no meaning apart from some moral sense. If God judges kindness to be better than cruelty, this must mean that God is benevolent, that is, has certain affections or dispositions. Balguy's objection to this is that we cannot suppose God to act from mere impulse: he acts from reason or understanding; it is not just that he happens to like kindness, but that he understands that kindness is good, that is, in accordance with the real nature or fitness of things. But, says Hutcheson, we cannot escape from what Balguy calls blind impulse. For what he seems to mean is that any ultimate end is a blind impulse and we cannot escape from supposing some ultimate end.

In saying this Hutcheson is, of course, merely putting forward the logico-psychological argument. It is clear, however, that Balguy is right in urging that the logico-psychological argument implies relativism. If actions can be justified ultimately only by reference to feelings or desires, it follows that right and wrong are relative to feelings and desires, whether human or divine.

Balguy's argument is not merely an *argumentum ad hominem* directed against Hutcheson, who was a Presbyterian minister before he became Professor of Philosophy at Glasgow. It might be thought that, if we do not postulate a God who is the sum of all perfections and so on, we need not worry even if Hutcheson's theory does lead to the conclusion that he must have a moral sense and that not all his actions can properly be called reasonable. It might be thought that this is a theological question which does not concern ethics. This would, however, be a mistake. The real point of Balguy's objection may be stated without bringing in God at all. For, according to Hutcheson, to say that something is good or bad, right or wrong, is just to say that men in general approve or disapprove of it. It follows that if human nature happened to be different, what is now right would be wrong and vice versa. This is not merely to say that what is now thought to be right would then be thought wrong. It is the much stronger assertion that what is now right would be wrong. In the days when men in general approved of torturing suspected criminals in order to make them confess, this procedure really was right; it has become wrong now only because our feelings have changed and may well become right again, if, as seems not unlikely, there should be a further change of attitude.

Again, let us suppose, not that the moral sense of mankind changes radically, but that there is just one tribe somewhere whose moral sense is quite different from that of most people. Let us suppose, for example, that they approve of skinning babies alive for sport. It has seemed to many that a consistent relativist confronted with such a tribe could not say that they were acting wrongly. He would, of course, feel a strong impulse to condemn such a practice. He would indeed disapprove of it because his moral sense would be different from theirs.

He could, then, according to his definition of 'wrong', say that their behaviour was wrong. But on reflection he would have to admit that they had an equal right to say that it was he who was wrong ('sentimental', 'squeamish') and they who were right. The question 'which is really right?' would be a meaningless one. To ask it would be like asking whether, apart from the traffic regulations of this or that country, it is really right to drive on the right-hand side of the road or the left. The answer here is, of course, that apart from a given traffic code this question has no meaning. In exactly the same way, it is meaningless to ask whether, apart from the conventions of this or that society, it is right or wrong to wear a black tie at a funeral or a white one at an examination. On a relativist view, it is argued, we would have to regard skinning babies alive in exactly the same way: as a practice that happened to be condemned in our society, but which very well might be approved in some other society. If this did happen, the appropriate attitude would seem to be: 'Well, well, how odd! But after all, they have their customs and we have ours.'

Hutcheson does make some attempt to answer this objection. He would be prepared to say that our hypothetical tribe had a sickly or degenerate moral sense, much as its members might all be colour blind. But if the moral sense itself may be sickly or healthy, there must be some way of knowing when a moral sense is healthy and when it is not. As Hutcheson himself asks: 'Must we not know, therefore, antecedently, what is morally good or evil by our reason, before we can know that our moral sense is right?'[1]

Hutcheson's own answer is to say, in effect, that we call certain men colour blind just because what they see is different from what most of their fellows see. The standard is the normal observer, which means the majority of observers. There is no need then to suppose that we can judge what colour a thing really has without reference to the sight at all: that a blind man

[1] *Essay on the Nature and Conduct of the Passions and Affections* (3rd ed. London, 1742), p. 286.

could work out by pure reason what colour it is and judge accordingly whether our eyes are in order or not. Our judgement of colour is necessarily relative to the sense of sight. To say that a thing is coloured is just to say that it causes certain colour sensations in a person with eyes of a certain kind. It is, however, convenient to take as the standard not our own eyesight, but that of the average human being.

It would follow from this that we are justified in condemning the moral judgement of our hypothetical tribe because it does not agree with the general consensus of mankind. Most of us, however, would want to say that an action may be right, even though most people think it wrong. To accept the general consensus of opinion as our ultimate criterion would be to accept a purely conventional morality.

The first objection to naturalism, then, is that it inevitably leads to relativism and that the relativist is bound to say either that there are no grounds for condemning a person whose moral judgements happen to be different from your own, or that the only ground for condemning him is the purely conventional one that he thinks differently from most people. Hutcheson himself seems to concede this point when he says: 'No man can immediately either approve or disapprove as morally good or evil his own moral sense'; and again: 'We should no more call the moral sense morally good or evil than we call the sense of tasting savoury or unsavoury, sweet or bitter.'[1] In other words, moral judgements arise only within a particular moral system, in which certain moral rules or axioms are presupposed. We cannot strictly speaking apply moral epithets to these axioms themselves. It follows that we cannot, strictly, say that one moral system is better or worse than another, or even that one is 'healthy' and the other 'degenerate'.

Strictly speaking, then, a Hitler or a Genghis Khan is no worse than a St Francis or a Gandhi. We can say only that each has a different morality, and that each would condemn the

[1] *Op. cit.* p. 239.

other. We cannot even raise the question whether one of these moralities is better than the other in any objective sense, though we can of course ask which happens to agree with our own morality, or with that of most men.

To many people this conclusion seems utterly outrageous, seems indeed to destroy morality altogether. It is, of course, none the worse for that, if it really is the conclusion to which the evidence seems to point. Others have maintained that the conclusion is not really as shocking as it seems at first sight. In this chapter I am stating the objection, not discussing it. It is important to realize, however, that this is the central objection to naturalism, and the one that lies behind most of the opposition to any kind of naturalist ethic. Any naturalist theory must certainly take account of it.

The second main traditional argument against naturalism is the one that I have referred to as the authority argument. It would generally be said that moral principles have authority over us. We may not always obey them, but we think it reasonable that they should take precedence over other principles, for example over maxims of self-interest, when the two conflict. According to Bishop Butler it is this authority or, as he also calls it, 'natural supremacy', that distinguishes conscience above all from the other parts of human nature. 'Had it strength as it had right; had it power as it had manifest authority, it would absolutely govern the world.'[1] Professor Baier puts the same point by saying that it is a rule of reason that moral reasons are superior to all other kinds of reason.

Now how can this authority be explained on a naturalist view of morality? There is no great problem if the naturalist is an egoist like Hobbes. According to him human beings have at bottom just one instinct, which may be conveniently called self-interest, and consequently just one ultimate aim, the gratification of desire. To say that X ought to be done is, when properly understood, to say that X will in the long run gratify one's desires better than any other alternative course of action.

[1] J. Butler, *Works*, ed. Samuel Halifax (London, 1834), vol. II, p. 45.

On this view the authority of morality is simply the authority of self-interest. And self-interest has authority simply because this is what human beings do, in fact, aim at. To make a moral judgement is to refer something to this basic human instinct. To ask whether the instinct itself is good does not really make sense: it is like asking if the sense of taste is bitter.

There is no great difficulty about this if one supposes that human beings have at bottom only one instinct. But there is a grave problem here for those naturalists who, like Shaftesbury and Hutcheson, maintained against Hobbes that men have at least two instincts, benevolence and self-interest, while agreeing with him that moral terms were properly to be regarded as expressions of a basic human instinct. They agreed, that is to say, that 'X ought to be done' is to be interpreted as 'X is a means to the end Y', where Y is set before human beings, as it were, by an instinct. If there are two basic instincts, self-love and benevolence, it will follow that there are two senses of the word 'ought'. 'X ought to be done' may mean 'X is a means to gratifying my own desires', or 'obtaining the most pleasure for myself in the long run', or, alternatively, it may mean 'X is a means to gratifying the desires of others' or 'obtaining the most pleasure for other people in the long run'. These will be, respectively, the ought of self-interest and the ought of altruism. Although he would not want to put it in terms of human instincts, much the same point is made by Baier when he says that there are two kinds of good reason for action: reasons of self-interest and reasons of benevolence. The difficulty is, of course, that once you say that there are two human instincts instead of one, the question at once arises: how do you judge between them?

If what we have here is just a conflict between feelings which people happen to have, the desire to seek one's own pleasure and the desire to further the interests of others, then there would seem to be no way of deciding between them except by asking which desire happens to be the stronger. There will no doubt be some people in whom self-interest is very much stronger than benevolence. There are others perhaps who care very little about themselves and are always much more concerned about the interests of others. No doubt most of us fall somewhere between these two: sometimes we desire to further our own interests, and sometimes we prefer to further the interests of others, according to the circumstances in each individual case. On a naturalist view these differences would seem to be a matter of individual temperament and not to call for any moral judgement at all. As Butler himself puts it:

Thus different men are, by their particular natures, hurried on to pursue honour or riches or pleasure: there are also persons whose temper leads them, in an uncommon degree, to kindness, compassion, doing good to their fellow creatures...Let everyone, then, quietly follow his nature; as passion, reflection, appetite, the several parts of it, happen to be strongest: but let not the man of virtue take upon him to blame the ambitious, the covetous, the dissolute; since these equally with him obey and follow their nature.[1]

This conclusion does not of course satisfy Butler, Shaftesbury, or Hutcheson. They are quite sure that men ought to follow the dictates of benevolence rather than those of self-interest, when these two conflict. But what, it may be asked, does 'ought' mean in this statement? Have we here the ought of self-interest or the ought of benevolence? Presumably not the first, since it could hardly be said that the way to attain one's own interest is to follow the dictates of benevolence rather than those of self-interest. Perhaps, then, the ought here is the ought of benevolence? This, however, will hardly do either. No doubt it is true that to follow the dictates of benevolence rather than those of self-interest is to attain the ends of benevolence. In itself, however, this would not give us a reason for preferring benevolence to self-interest, for one could equally say, using the other sense of 'ought', that one ought to prefer self-interest to benevolence.

Perhaps, then, we have here a third sense of 'ought' which is neither the ought of self-interest nor of benevolence? This was precisely what Shaftesbury, Butler and Hutcheson were driven to say. Consequently they postulated a third instinct,

---

[1] *Op. cit.* p. 39.

equally basic in human nature, which they called conscience or the moral sense, and which has the express function of mediating between the other two instincts when they conflict. This does not, however, really solve the problem. We have seen that to say that self-interest ought (using the ought of self-interest) to have precedence over benevolence, while true in this sense of 'ought', does not give a good reason for actually preferring self-interest to benevolence. Similarly to say that benevolence ought (using the ought of benevolence) to prevail over self-interest does not give a good reason for preferring benevolence to self-interest. By the same reasoning it is obvious that to say that the dictates of morality ought to prevail over those of either benevolence or self-interest, while no doubt true so long as ought means 'is a means to the ends set before us by the moral sense' (whatever they may be), does not give a good reason for preferring morality to either benevolence or self-interest. The naturalist, indeed, by insisting on analysing 'ought' in the way he does, has made it impossible for us to use the word so as to provide a final reason of the kind we are looking for. According to him 'I ought to do X' is to be interpreted as 'X is a means to an end which I actually have'. This does enable us to choose between desires so long as our conflicting desires can be regarded as all aiming at the same broad end: for example, the maximum of pleasure in the long run or something of that kind. If, however, we have more than one broad end of this kind, all that would seem to follow is that the word 'ought' has more than one sense. It would not seem to be possible to say meaningfully that we ought to choose one end rather than another, unless indeed these alternative ends can be regarded as really means to some more ultimate end.

The non-naturalist philosophers who argued against Hutcheson put this point by saying that the faculty which has the function of choosing between feelings cannot itself be a feeling. So long as the moral sense is simply one desire alongside others, there can be no possible reason why it should have priority over those others. This will remain true even if the moral sense is regarded as a desire that one kind of desire (benevolence) should prevail over another kind (self-interest). There is no reason why this desire should be gratified rather than those which conflict with it, unless indeed it is a stronger desire than those others. What most moralists want to say is that conscience should prevail over conflicting feelings, even if it is not stronger than those feelings. On the naturalist analysis this statement would not seem to make sense.

It might perhaps be said, in reply to this, that the moral sense has at least as much authority as self-interest. For self-interest does have authority and not merely power. It is certainly not true that we always do what will make for our interests in the long run. Very often we yield to the impulse to gratify the desire of the moment, even though we realize that this will be to our disadvantage in the long run. One cannot say, then, that self-interest (that is, what Butler calls 'cool self love', the desire to do what is to our ultimate advantage) is invariably stronger than the individual desires which compete with it. Self-interest does not always have power over these desires; it does have authority, in the sense that while we may well yield to the individual desire when it conflicts with self-interest, we will feel, on reflection, that we ought not to allow the desire to triumph over self-interest. In precisely the same way, it may be argued, we do sometimes allow self-interest to triumph over moral principles which conflict with it; but on reflection we feel that we ought not to have done this. In Butler's language, the individual desires ('affections', 'passions') are subordinate to cool self-love and (though it is not clear that Butler does say this without qualification) cool self-love is in its turn subordinate to conscience. Since no one disputes that the urge to attain the greatest advantage in the long run is simply a desire which human beings happen to have, it must be admitted that it is possible for such a desire to have authority as distinct from power. Consequently the authority of conscience is no obstacle to regarding it as just the feeling, or set of feelings, that human beings happen to have.

What, however, is meant by saying that we feel, on reflection, that we ought to follow the dictates of enlightened self-interest rather than yield to the desire of the moment? We are not prepared to count anything as being to our advantage in the long run unless we think that on reflection we would prefer it to the alternative. And to say that we prefer it is not just to say that we think that we ought to give it precedence over this or that desire. 'Prefer' here means something like 'gives us more pleasure' or 'satisfies more desires' or 'satisfies a more central desire'. There is a sense then in which the authority of self-interest can be reduced to power after all. Butler was, of course, quite right in pointing out that self-interest is not always stronger than some particular desire at a given moment. But if we look beyond the moment to a man's more settled and permanent desires, we find that it is those which are more permanent and enduring, more central to his total satisfaction, that it is in his interest to gratify. That indeed is just what we mean by self-interest. Now, it has sometimes been claimed that morality is like self-interest in this respect: that moral impulses are more central to the self (perhaps to 'the real self') and the source of greater and more permanent satisfaction than those other desires which compete with them. One objection to this view is that ultimately it obliterates the distinction between morality and self-interest; indeed it must do so if self-interest means what we have just said that it means. There is also another and more obvious objection. We usually distinguish between what we prefer to do and what we think that we ought (morally) to do; and when we make this distinction we are not thinking simply of the preferences of the moment. We may sometimes feel that it is necessary to forgo some of our most settled and permanent desires in the interests of morality. We may feel this even if we are not, in fact, strong-willed enough actually to forgo these desires. Here it can hardly be said that the desire in question is in any sense less powerful than the moral impulse. Yet we still feel that here the moral impulse has authority, though not power.

Other Arguments against Naturalism

It seems, then, that the argument about authority does have considerable force against naturalism. Along with the point about relativism it constitutes a serious objection which any naturalist must meet fairly. There is also a third objection of a rather different kind. If morality is ultimately reducible to feelings of approval, it is obviously necessary to say with some precision just what these feelings are and how they differ from desires. This is necessary, not merely in the interests of clarity, but also to allay the suspicion that what are called feelings of approval are not really feelings or attitudes at all.

The eighteenth-century moralists regarded conscience, benevolence and self-interest as all human faculties, or dispositions, parts of human nature. There is, however, one obvious difference between conscience (or 'the moral sense') and the other two. Self-interest can be regarded as the desire to gain the maximum possible pleasure or satisfaction in the long run. Benevolence can be regarded as the desire that others shall gain the maximum possible pleasure or satisfaction in the long run. The moral sense, however, is not parallel to these. If it is a desire, we may ask what is it the desire for. If it is the desire to do what is right, then it is clear that 'right' means something other than 'approved by the moral sense'. Hutcheson, at least, was inclined to say that the moral sense always gave its vote on the side of benevolence when benevolence and self-interest came into conflict. But in that case the moral sense would seem to be simply a desire for the good of others and as such would not be different from benevolence. The moral sense, then, would seem to be not a desire but a tendency to approve of some desires and to disapprove of others. But the concept of approval is far from clear. It has often been argued that to approve of X really means to think that X is good. If this is true, then it is clear that the naturalists are quite wrong in attempting to define good in terms of approval.

While I have put these problems in terms of the eighteenth-century controversy, it is quite clear that the same essential difficulties confront naturalism today. We no longer feel it appropriate to talk of Self-interest, Benevolence and Conscience as parts or faculties of the human soul. Any naturalist today, however, still needs to answer at least these three questions:

1. Does naturalism imply relativism and can relativism be defended?

2. Can naturalism account for the authority which it is generally felt does attach to moral principles?

3. If morality is to be explained in terms of pro-attitudes or feelings of approval, is it possible to give a coherent account of those attitudes without presupposing moral concepts?

In what follows I shall be attempting to answer these questions.

CHAPTER 10

THE DEFENCE OF
RELATIVISM

To many people it seems obvious that a relativist theory of morals not only fails to do justice to our most elementary moral concepts, but is itself grossly immoral and likely to lead to cynicism and loose living in those who adopt it. The naturalist, as we have seen, is ultimately forced to admit, with Hutcheson, that it does not make sense to apply moral epithets to the moral sense itself, any more than to call the sense of taste bitter or sweet. It seems to follow from this that if A and B have different fundamental attitudes, it does not make sense to say that one of them has the right attitudes, and the other the wrong ones. Thus, if A happens to prefer to be kind to other people and B happens to prefer to be cruel to them, it is just as if one happened to have a taste for beer and the other happened to have a taste for whisky. In terms of our earlier example, there is no rational ground for saying that the tribe which happens to enjoy skinning babies alive for sport is misguided or in any way worse than we are. Naturally we think that they are wrong, but equally naturally they think that they are right. Neither we nor they can be properly said to be really right or wrong.

The relativist, however, may reasonably object to this conclusion. To talk of 'really' right and 'really' wrong is to assume an objectivist standpoint which he explicitly repudiates. When a consistent relativist says that an action is wrong, he means nothing more than this, that it is not in accordance with the fundamental moral principles which he himself adopts. According to this definition, the behaviour of our hypothetical tribe is wrong. Moreover, the naturalist will say, his analysis of 'wrong' is the correct one, the one which underlies everybody's use of the word, including the objectivist's, whether he realizes this or not. Consequently the skinning of babies is wrong simply and without qualification. There is no other sense in which it can be said to be 'not really wrong'.

The implications of this reply are worth considering. It is sometimes thought that relativism makes for tolerance. It is said, for example, that the twentieth-century anthropologist is much better equipped to deal with a primitive people than the nineteenth-century missionary, just because the anthropologist realizes that moral beliefs are a function of a culture. If we happen to be born into a particular society at a particular time, we can hardly help believing that (say) slavery is right; if into a different society, or into the same society at a different time, we can hardly help believing that it is wrong. The missionary did not realize this; consequently when he was shocked and revolted by some native practices, he tried to alter them. The anthropologist, though he feels the same inclination to be shocked and revolted, realizes that these feelings are merely the result of his own prejudices and have no more objective validity than the natives' quite different feelings.

Many people are attracted to relativism because they prefer the attitude of the anthropologist to that of the missionary. It is not, however, really consistent to conclude from these premises that the missionary was wrong to react as he did. Tolerance does not really follow from relativism. For, if moral judgements are really the reflections of our culture, they will continue to reflect our culture, whether we realize that fact or not. If, on the other hand, to realize that a moral judgement is merely the reflection of culture is to deny the soundness of the judgement, then it would seem to follow, not that all moral judgements reflect the culture, but only that unsound ones do.

There are two ways in which the anthropologist's argument may be put. It may be said that, as Hutcheson admitted, moral judgements are always relative to a set of basic assumptions or attitudes and that consequently it does not make sense to say that these attitudes themselves are good or bad. It makes sense to say 'I approve of X', but not to say 'My approving of

X is good' or 'Your disapproving of X is bad'. It follows from this, however, that it equally makes no sense to say 'I approve of neither approving nor disapproving of my approval of X'.

Alternatively, it may be said that moral judgements are ultimately expressions of desire and that one man's desire is not to be preferred to another's simply on the grounds that it is his. It follows that we ought not to prefer one moral judgement to another. But what is the status of the premise 'One man's desire is not to be preferred to another's simply on the grounds that it is his'? It seems clear that this is being put forward as an objective moral principle. As such, of course, it is not one that the relativist can consistently appeal to. The relativist clearly cannot say that we ought not to approve of A's attitude simply because we happen to share it; for, according to him, there is no other ground on which we ought to do anything. The only ultimate moral principle is that I ought to do whatever is in accordance with certain attitudes of mind. This is, indeed, an analytic statement; it is what 'ought' means. Clearly we cannot both hold this and go on to assert that I ought not to prefer my own attitudes to those of other people simply because they are mine. Morality consists in acting in accordance with certain attitudes just because they happen to be my attitudes. If 'right' and 'wrong' really mean what accords with, or conflicts with, our desires, then it follows that we do condemn those whose desires or attitudes differ from our own. If this argument is sound, the relativist can no longer claim that his meta-ethic leads to tolerance. But he is equally exonerated from the charge that he is committed to tolerating evil and that his analysis of moral judgements does away with morality altogether. To say that my approval or disapproval is relative to certain fundamental assumptions or attitudes of mine does not prevent it from being genuinely approval or disapproval.

It may be objected that the premise in the argument which we have been criticizing is wrongly stated as 'one ought not to prefer one man's desires to another's on that ground alone'.

What is being said is rather that there is no valid *reason* for preferring one man's desires to another's. The principle is not one of morals, but of logic; a better statement of it would be that desires are not capable of being true or false.

Now there seems little doubt that the principle is in fact often interpreted as a moral principle. The anthropologist who condemns the missionary means that we *ought* to be tolerant of value judgements that differ from our own. The inconsistencies of some relativists need not, however, invalidate relativism. Is the statement that there is no reason to prefer one man's desires to another's really inconsistent with relativism? I have suggested that, according to the relativist, the only ground for preferring anything to anything is that it is the desire of one man, namely myself; but this, it may be argued, is beside the point. After all, if I like oysters and you like mussels, I have an excellent reason for buying oysters and for encouraging oyster culture. And I have no reason for buying mussels or encouraging mussel culture; but this need not prevent me from admitting that you have an equally good reason for buying mussels and that there is no sense in which my taste can be regarded as better than yours, or in which I can be said to be right in my preferences and you to be wrong in yours.

The argument here is that my taste for oysters provides a reason for doing anything that may lead to the gratification of that desire, but not for calling your taste for mussels wrong. This, however, is not nearly as obvious as it seems. There is, to begin with, the difficulty that calling your taste wrong and persuading you that it is wrong may be a very effective means of enabling me to gratify my taste. According to some relativists, this is an exact parallel to what does happen in moral disputes. If I happen to have a taste for a quiet life and you happen to have a taste for strenuous heroism, each of us tries to persuade the other that his taste is wrong. And why not, if 'wrong' merely means 'what conflicts with my tastes'?

Well, it may be answered, that an activity is not to *your* taste is no reason for me to give it up, if it accords with *my* taste.

True; but, since tastes may change, and most men are imitative and impressionable, you may change your taste if you find it different from your neighbours'. People do, after all, acquire a quite genuine taste for caviare, or for dry sherry, as the result of social pressure. And there may be social reasons why it is inconvenient for us to have different tastes. If a husband likes to take his holidays in the mountains, and his wife by the sea, he may well try to induce her to change her tastes. He will do this by dwelling on the joys of mountain scenery, and the discomforts of the seaside. Certainly, this is an attempt to persuade his wife that she, too, really prefers the mountains, not (she knows this only too well already) that *he* does. But what one 'really' wants, 'at bottom', is not very clearly distinguished from what one may come to want, if one looks at the alternatives 'in a fresh light'. It is at least conceivable that words like 'right' and 'wrong' arise out of the constant endeavour to induce others to share one's taste for (let us say) a peaceable life, in which one can rely on the co-operation of one's neighbour.

The point at the moment is that the word 'wrong' is ambiguous. It may mean morally wrong or it may mean erroneous, as when we tell a schoolboy that his answer is wrong. And no doubt I am entitled to call a taste that conflicts with my own morally wrong if morality is ultimately a matter of taste, but I am not entitled to call it erroneous. That is what is meant by saying that desires are not capable of being true or false. Very well. But it follows that I am, after all, perfectly justified in condemning you because of your taste for mussels. Or, the missionary can, in spite of the anthropologist, quite legitimately accuse the natives of being sunk in sin. The only thing neither of us can do is to accuse our opponents of an intellectual error. And it is seldom that the righteously indignant want to do this.

What the argument really depends on is the principle that false beliefs, and false beliefs only, are to be rejected. This is, as it were, a self-regulating principle of science; one might almost say, in Kant's terms, an autonomous principle of reason. Nevertheless, it is not in itself a scientific belief; it is not itself capable of being true or false; it is a procedural rule which the scientist adopts for his own purposes. It is only by erecting this principle into a self-evident moral axiom which, it is maintained, the relativist cannot but accept, that it is possible to argue that the relativist is not justified in condemning those whose fundamental moral attitudes differ from his own. There seems no reason, however, why the relativist should adopt this moral axiom. Indeed to adopt it seems clearly inconsistent with relativism.

But, it will be asked, isn't relativism itself then condemned by its inability to accommodate a principle that is clearly both right and rational? Consider the following dialogue:

A. Why do you consider this course of conduct wrong?

B. Ultimately because it conflicts with certain fundamental attitudes that I happen to have.

A. You realize, don't you, that other people may have different fundamental attitudes?

B. Certainly.

A. In that case they will consider right the course of conduct which you think wrong?

B. Yes, of course.

A. They are, then, just as much entitled to follow their own beliefs as you are to follow yours?

B. No.

A. Why not?

B. Just because their attitudes and beliefs are different from mine.

A. And there is no other reason? There is no objective ground on which you can say that your attitudes are to be preferred to theirs?

B. No.

If that is the position that the relativist is reduced to, then, it will be said, he has clearly demonstrated his arrogance, his intolerance and, indeed, his irrationality. Moreover, his moral system is bound to be internally inconsistent. At some stage in the conduct of his life he will find, if he is a reasonable man, that he needs to make the distinction that we all make between those matters of taste in which each man is at liberty to follow his own fancy, and those matters in which we expect a man to adhere to some objective standards. The principle that a man is not to be condemned merely because his tastes happen to differ from our own is not one that can readily be dispensed with. The relativist will find himself adopting it at one point in his system; if then he renounces it at another point, he is clearly guilty of inconsistency.

This is a formidable indictment and may well seem utterly convincing at first sight. On consideration, however, it may prove to be less so.

Is it, after all, true that one is not justified in condemning a man because his fundamental attitudes differ from one's own? Suppose I say that X is cruel, selfish and unkind. Does not this amount to saying that his attitudes to other people and to their desires are different from mine? It is just because they are different from one's own that one dislikes and avoids people who have such attitudes. What more is necessary, according to the objectivist, before one is justified in condemning such people? The objectivist will presumably say that it is necessary that cruelty, unkindness, etc., should be objectively wrong and that one's own opposing attitudes should be objectively right. This would suggest, however, that the cruel man is guilty of intellectual error, that he has a mistaken belief about what is objectively right. And it is not for intellectual error that one condemns him. Indeed it is a principle, quite as firmly based as the principle that one ought not to condemn a man simply because his desires differ from one's own, that one ought not to condemn a man for an honest intellectual error.

The objectivist may retort that he condemns the cruel man, not because he is honestly mistaken about what is right and what is wrong, but because, knowing this as well as any of the rest of us, he fails to act on his beliefs. This does not, however, enable him to meet the objection. According to the objectivist, presumably, it is objectively wrong not to do what one believes to be right. Is the cruel man at fault, then, because he does not realize the truth of this proposition? If so, it is still for an intellectual error that he is being condemned. If not, then it is hard to see how the alleged objective truth or falsity of moral propositions is relevant here at all. What the wrongdoer is being condemned for is his weakness of will, perhaps, or his refusal to regard moral truths as important and as furnishing a guide to conduct. These would seem to be attitudes: the kind of fundamental moral attitude that the relativist regards as the ultimate criterion for moral judgement. It would seem that, in practice if not in theory, the objectivist adopts the same criteria: that he condemns a man simply because he has certain fundamental attitudes which the objectivist himself does not share. If the objectivist denies this and insists that what he condemns a man for is his failure to believe certain fundamental moral truths, then he is clearly condemning for intellectual error. And, as we have said, to condemn a man for making an intellectual error is just as objectionable as to condemn him for not sharing our own attitudes.

It is clear from this that the objectivist is equally open to the charge of inconsistency. At some point in his moral system he will presumably adopt the principle that a man is not to be condemned for making an honest mistake about a matter of fact. Just as, at some point in *his* system, the relativist will be forced to adopt the principle that a man is not to be condemned merely because his desires differ from one's own. If it is inconsistent for the relativist to refuse to apply this principle to those fundamental attitudes or desires which form the basis of morality, it is equally inconsistent for the objectivist to refuse to apply the parallel principle to those fundamental beliefs about matters of moral fact which he regards as the basis of morality.

It would seem that, whether we regard wrongdoing as ultimately the holding of mistaken beliefs, or as the possession of attitudes differing from our own, we will have to make a distinction between those mistaken beliefs which do provide grounds for condemnation and those which do not, or, alternatively, between those differences in attitudes which provide grounds for condemnation and those which do not. The relativist does, of course, regard a taste for oysters, as against a taste for mussels, as quite different in this respect from a taste for cruelty as against a taste for kindness. Moral attitudes, he must say, provide ground for condemnation; non-moral attitudes do not. This is at least no more irrational than to say that mistakes about moral facts provide ground for condemnation, whereas mistakes about non-moral facts do not. It is not clear, indeed, that it is irrational at all.

If the relativist's position appears to be more irrational than it is, this may be, at least in part, because of the rigid line that is commonly drawn, in modern discussion, between subjectivism and naturalism. The subjectivist is commonly taken to be saying that ultimate moral attitudes are quite arbitrary, that they are just those that a man happens to have, and that no moral principle, however trivial or eccentric, need be debarred from serving as the fundamental one on which moral reasoning is based. There may be subjectivists who hold this, and it is indeed possible that subjectivists are ultimately forced to concede something like this, as a logical possibility. When subjectivist moral theories have been seriously advanced, however, they have almost always been combined with naturalism. The naturalist does not say that moral attitudes are arbitrary. He has usually said that they arise out of human nature, meaning by this that they are based on certain fairly constant human characteristics, such as a distaste for physical pain and a reliance on the help and encouragement of one's fellow-men. There are certain psychological and social facts, that is to say, which cause men to develop the attitudes that they do have. Moral attitudes have a definite role to play in human behaviour. As Hobbes would put it, it is by developing these attitudes that men are able to attain their ends in a world in which they need the co-operation and sympathy of other men. This does not rule out the possibility of some variations between individuals and between societies in their fundamental moral attitudes. It does, however, mean that in practice these variations will be restricted within at least some limits. This is why we feel that there is something odd about the suggestion that anything at all could serve as a fundamental moral principle.

The same consideration helps to dispose of another common objection to relativism. According to the relativist there is no rational way of deciding between two men who genuinely differ in their fundamental moral attitudes. We are disposed to resist this conclusion because we know that in practice we can, and do, settle moral disagreements by rational means. This is, however, easily explicable if human beings are, in fact, subject to very much the same pressures and motivated by many of the same basic desires, so that there is a stock of constant attitudes to which we can appeal with confidence. This applies particularly, of course, to people in the same community (between whom moral arguments are most likely to occur) whose moral attitudes have been moulded by the same social causes.

None of this, of course, affects the logical point. It is of course at least logically possible that men may differ in their fundamental moral attitudes. The relativist is committed to saying that, when this does occur, each will condemn the other and will condemn him, in the last analysis, for not sharing his own attitudes. The relativist need not say that a man's ultimate moral assumptions are arbitrarily assumed by him: they are forced upon him by a combination of psychological and social causes. They need not be irrational either: most men will feel an urge to make their moral attitudes consistent with one another and with their beliefs about such matters of fact as may be relevant. Nevertheless, a system of moral reasoning, like any other system, depends ultimately on certain basic assumptions which must just be taken for granted. For moral systems these assumptions are, according to the naturalist, attitudes which he does not indeed just happen to have, but which he comes to have, and by which he guides his life. On the basis of these attitudes he approves and condemns. If there is anything irrational or unjust about this, it is not made less so by supposing these basic assumptions to be beliefs about matters of moral fact. For, in the first case, there is the difficulty that it is hard to see how a belief about a matter of fact can be in itself a ground for action; secondly, it is, to say the least, no more rational to condemn or approve another man because he differs from us in his belief about a matter of fact, than it is to approve or condemn him because he differs from us in his emotional attitudes.

CHAPTER II

THE AUTHORITY OF CONSCIENCE

As we have seen, the second traditional objection to naturalism is that it cannot account for the authority of conscience, that the faculty which enables us to judge between feelings cannot itself be a feeling. Since I have discussed this objection mainly in the terms used in the eighteenth century, I shall, before giving the naturalist's reply, briefly re-state the objection in more modern terms.

According to the naturalist, moral sentiments (pro- and anti-attitudes) are just feelings that men happen to have. Men have other sentiments as well (for example, those which we lump together under the name of self-interest) and it is conceded that moral sentiments often conflict with these. When they do conflict, why should moral sentiments take precedence?

Moreover, what is meant by saying that they take precedence? Not that men do always follow the moral course rather than the interested one when the two conflict, because clearly men do not always do this. Does it mean, then, that they *ought* to take the moral course? But what, then, does 'ought' mean here? If 'I ought to do X' means 'I have a moral sentiment in favour of doing X', then of course I ought to do what I have a moral sentiment towards doing. This is analytic. But 'I ought to do what I have a moral sentiment towards doing' would not then be a reason for preferring moral sentiments to others.

The problem, then, for the naturalist is this. According to him 'I ought to do X' means 'I have a special kind of pro-attitude towards doing X'. What now would 'I ought to allow my moral sentiments to prevail over my other sentiments when they conflict' mean? Presumably it would mean 'I have the same kind of pro-attitude towards allowing my moral sentiments to prevail'.

Now there are two possibilities here:

The Authority of Conscience

(a) There may be no contradiction in saying *both* 'I have a pro-attitude towards doing X' and 'I have an anti-attitude towards allowing this attitude to prevail over other attitudes'.

(b) There may be a contradiction between these two.

Suppose (a). Then there is no contradiction in saying 'I ought to do X; but I ought not to do what I ought to do when what I ought to do conflicts with a desire'. (I have a pro-attitude of a special kind towards doing X; but I also have a pro-attitude of the same kind towards repressing such pro-attitudes when they conflict with desires.) But if there is no contradiction in saying this, it becomes an empirical question whether conscience has authority or not. Moreover, the question is simply whether, as a matter of fact, men do have a pro-attitude (of this special kind) towards letting their pro-attitudes (of this kind) prevail over their desires or not.

It may be, of course, that a pro-attitude always does give rise to a higher-order pro-attitude towards letting the pro-attitude prevail over conflicting desires. But it would seem to be also true that a desire gives rise to a higher-order desire that the desire should prevail against any conflicting sentiments. In short, the question Ought the pro-attitude or the desire to prevail? arises at this second-order level. And if we take 'ought' here to mean 'Is there a third-order pro-attitude towards letting the second-order pro-attitude prevail?' then no doubt a third-order desire arises to confront it. And so on, for ever.

It seems clear from this that the analysis I have given of 'I ought to let my moral sentiments prevail' is not an adequate one. What we mean by this is not just that I have a higher-order pro-attitude. For this would not answer the question 'Am I to let the desire or the pro-attitude prevail?' And 'I ought to let the pro-attitude prevail' is an answer to this question.

Well, it may be said, of course this analysis is defective. 'Ought' is not merely the expression of a particular type of attitude: it has imperative force. 'My moral sentiments ought to prevail', then, means 'Let my moral sentiments prevail', which is an answer to the 'Am I to...' question.

The Defence of Naturalism

But this does not solve the problem. For there is a sense in which 'I desire X' also gives rise to an imperative. As it is often put, that I desire to do something is a reason for doing it. So that, on this view, we would have two conflicting imperatives opposing each other just as, on the other, we had two opposing sentiments.

Now suppose (b). Then there is a contradiction in saying 'I ought to do X; but I ought not to do what I ought to do when what I ought to do conflicts with a desire'. If this is logically and not merely empirically impossible, then it must be part of the meaning of 'a moral attitude' that it is one that ought to prevail over all other attitudes. There are two possibilities here. To say that it ought to prevail may be just to say that it is an attitude of a certain kind; in which case we must say, as before, that 'this attitude ought to prevail' is not an answer to the question 'Am I to let it prevail?' Alternatively, to say that it is a moral attitude is not just to say that it is an attitude of a certain kind; which is to abandon the naturalist analysis of 'ought'.

We must conclude, then, that, whether we say that it is logically or merely empirically impossible for moral principles not to have authority, the naturalist analysis of moral principles cannot account for this authority. Notice that there are two separate points here: (1) If a moral sentiment is just one feeling alongside others, which may conflict with it, there seems no reason why it ought to prevail over those others. (2) If the naturalist analysis is correct, we cannot even state that it ought to prevail over those others. For this would mean 'I have a particular kind of pro-attitude in favour of its prevailing'. And this is not what is meant.

There is, it seems to me, one way and one way only in which the naturalist may meet this difficulty.

In choosing between conflicting desires or attitudes, men do evolve certain principles. That is to say, they develop habits of choice. When they are influenced by conflicting considerations, they make decisions about which consideration outweighs the other. Such decisions are not always consciously and deliberately made, and of course they are influenced by the mores of the community. But, surveying a man's behaviour over a period, we (or he himself) can find certain patterns, or principles, in it: for example, that he always tells the truth unless by so doing he will hurt someone's feelings.

It is not necessary to suppose that he consciously formulates such principles to himself, or that he would be able to give any very coherent account of what considerations are, for him, 'over-riding' or 'final'. The process of moral deliberation may appear to him very much as Ross described it, as a more or less intuitive 'weighing' of different considerations until he finally decides that one or the other of the alternative courses of action is the right one. But such an account is clearly incomplete. The metaphor of 'weighing' presupposes some scale on which values are read off, some criteria (whether consciously realized or not) according to which the alternatives are compared. Unless he is quite unusually inconsistent, completely at the mercy of the last book or newspaper leader he has read, or the last sermon or political speech he has heard, these criteria will be relatively constant. It is this fact that enables us to make judgements of character: to say '*X* is a thorough-going liberal' or '*Y* is fundamentally puritanical' or 'Mrs *Z* is concerned only with what the neighbours will think'. The suggestion is, then, that the principles or criteria by which a man regulates his life constitute his morality.

If we now ask what is meant by saying that moral principles have authority over any other principles, the answer is quite simple. For any man there must be some principles that have authority in this sense, some principles which he habitually follows when he is faced with a conflict of ends. Whatever these principles may be constitute his moral principles; because that is just what the word 'moral' means.

It may be objected that in that case his moral principles will have power over him, rather than authority. It is necessary to amend the definition in order to meet this objection. Every man will have principles of this kind which he generally follows or at least thinks of himself as following. When he departs from them, he feels guilt and remorse.

On this view, to say that moral principles ought to prevail over, say, self-interest, is certainly to say that the speaker has a pro-attitude in favour of allowing moral principles to triumph over self-interest. This statement, however, now becomes analytic, since he means by 'moral principles' whatever principles he prefers before all others which may conflict with them. It is possible, of course, that he might prefer that maxims of self-interest should prevail over any principles which might conflict with them. In that case, we would say that his morality was a purely selfish one. To say that an attitude is a moral one is indeed to say that it is an attitude of a certain kind: it is that kind of attitude which I prefer to prevail over others. Consequently, in saying that it is an attitude of that kind I am automatically answering the question 'Am I to let it prevail?'

One objection to this solution will be that it does plainly involve us in relativism. This objection has, however, been discussed in the last chapter. A more pertinent objection at this point is that this definition of morality is not in accordance with the way in which we actually use moral terms. Some philosophers insist that we can define morality only by reference to its content. Only principles which lay down certain rules, or rules about a certain type of subject, are, they would say, properly moral rules. Others are not moral, however central they may be in the lives of the people who follow them, and even if the failure to follow them should be accompanied by remorse and guilt. Other philosophers, while prepared to rule out content and to define moral principles purely in terms of their form, would nevertheless insist that there are some kinds of principle which are not moral even if they do have authority over a particular person. In particular, it is often claimed that maxims of self-interest cannot also be moral principles. 'To act on the principle of furthering one's own interests and ignoring everyone else's is a perfectly possible and, in a sense, rational thing to do; but it is not to act on a moral principle, for the word "moral" excludes such behaviour.'[1] The reason usually given for this exclusion is that maxims of self-interest cannot be universalized.

I shall be discussing the definition of morality in general and universalizability in particular in the following chapters. At the moment I shall merely say that the definition of morality just put forward is at least consistent with one common use of the word.

We can speak quite intelligibly of the morality of Satan; meaning thereby the principles which Satan consistently follows as his over-riding ones, even though in content these principles would presumably differ quite drastically from our own. It is true that Satan's principles must, at least, have the same subject-matter as our own: that is to say, they would be concerned with the pleasure and pain of sentient beings. They might, however, be completely selfish. And I think that, if we did discover some-one who felt guilt and remorse about matters which seemed to us to have nothing to do with morality at all, we would still have to regard his attitudes on these subjects as moral attitudes.

It is true, of course, that there is another sense of the word 'morality' in which we would say that the code of conduct followed by Satan was not a morality at all, but rather the nega-tion of all morality. We might also say of the thorough-going egoist, not that his morality was a purely selfish one, but that he followed self-interest to the exclusion of all morality. I do not want to say that one of these uses is correct and the other in-correct. The meaning of a word is what it is generally used to mean; and both these uses are standard in English. The point is that normally when we use the word 'morality' we have both these uses in mind and do not distinguish between them. That is to say, we normally think of a man's moral principles as both having authority over him, and as having a certain content.

We have here, in short, an instance of a very common class of terms, terms which connote more than one characteristic.

[1] J. Kemp in 'Foundations of Morality', *Philosophical Quarterly* (October 1957), p. 316.

They are able to do so because normally these characteristics occur together. Consequently we do not need to ask ourselves which of these characteristics we have principally in mind, or whether we would continue to use the term if only one of the characteristics were present, and not both. The stock example is the one about the man who went round the tree containing a squirrel and who may or may not have gone round the squirrel, since it ran round the tree away from him. There is a less hackneyed example, which I take from Hart and Honoré,[1] and which may seem less trivial since it is able to borrow the dignity of the law. A man standing on one side of the State boundary between North Carolina and Tennessee shot and killed a man who was standing on the other side. Did the murder take place in North Carolina or in Tennessee? This was an important question legally because it had to be answered before it could be determined which State had legal authority to try the case.

It is usual to cite such examples in order to make the point that what looks like a question of fact may very well turn out to be a purely verbal question involving a decision. My point, however, is a slightly different one. In both these examples we have instances of a very common class of terms, terms which connote more than one characteristic. They are able to do so because normally these characteristics occur together. We take it for granted that if we are first north, then east, then south, then west, and then again north of the squirrel, we will also have been first in front of him, then to the right of him, then behind him, then on his left, and finally in front again. Since these two types of squirrel circumambulation normally occur together, we do not need to ask ourselves which of them we have in mind when we say that we have gone round the squirrel. We could say that we mean either, or both, or indeed neither. Either, because we will readily accept either analysis if somebody puts it to us as the meaning of 'go round'. Both, because, having accepted one analysis, we will readily admit, if the other is put

---

[1] H. L. A. Hart and A. M. Honoré, *Causation in the Law* (Oxford, Clarendon Press, 1959), p. 87 n. The case is *State of North Carolina v. Hall*, 1894.

to us, that we do mean that as well. Neither, because in fact when we use a term like 'go round' we do not have any analysis specifically in mind: we are referring to a common enough phenomenon which we know by experience and which we presume that our hearers will know by experience also. In the same way, we take it for granted that the State in which the murderer happens to be at the time of his crime will also be the State in which his victim is. For that matter it is also the State in which the bullet is, or in which the flash of the gun is, or the smoke from the barrel, or the blood dripping on the ground. We may easily be brought to admit that, when we say that the murder took place somewhere, we imply that all of these things occurred there. But we might not be able to say which of these we had principally in mind. Some of them, indeed, may not have been in our minds at all when we uttered the phrase.

The importance of these peculiar cases is that they demonstrate that the connection between the various characteristics connoted by the same term, though usual, is not invariable. This is important because it may help us to see something else: that, even if the connection were invariable, it might still be contingent and not necessary. It is perhaps necessarily true that if a murder takes place at X, then the *victim* is at X when the murder takes place. Or it is perhaps necessarily true that if a murder takes place at X the *murderer* is at X when the murder takes place. The court which decided the case I have mentioned presumably decided, among other things, which of these statements is analytic and which synthetic. But even if it were never necessary to make such a decision, even if murderers and their victims always were in the same State, that they were always in the same State would be a contingent and not a necessary fact. Suppose that I define 'water' as H_2O and also as a liquid with a boiling-point of 100 °C. That water is a compound of hydrogen and oxygen is an analytic statement. It is also an analytic statement that water has a boiling-point of 100 °C. But it is, of course, synthetic that this particular compound of hydrogen and oxygen has this particular boiling-point.

In the same way it is, I suggest, analytic that moral rules have authority over other rules when they conflict. It is also, no doubt, analytic that moral rules are, say, those embodying the point of view of an impartial, dispassionate observer. We normally use the term morality so as to connote both of these characteristics. We are justified in doing so because, as a matter of fact, most of us do guide our lives by principles which do embody the point of view of an impartial, dispassionate observer. Nevertheless, it is a synthetic, and not an analytic, statement that the rules which for us have authority are rules of this kind. We may well find someone for whom the rules which have authority are of a different kind: for example, maxims of self-interest. And, if we do, we may indeed say, if we like, 'Those just aren't moral rules by definition'. But we must not say 'Those aren't the rules which have authority over you, not the principles you take as final, not what you think you *ought* to do'. For, on a naturalist view, to take a rule as final is to think that one ought to follow it.

I would suggest, then, that the problem about the authority of conscience is based on a misapprehension. It is empirically true that principles of a certain kind do have authority over nearly all of us. This can be explained simply enough on psychological and sociological grounds. Philosophers have, however, commonly supposed it to be necessarily true that principles of just this kind should have authority over us. This cannot, of course, be explained on any naturalist theory. It is doubtful indeed whether it can be explained by a non-naturalist either. There is, however, no need to explain it if what has just been said is correct.

It is possible that some modern naturalists have fallen into the same trap. Russell, for example, distinguishes between personal desires, such as my desire to have a glass of wine with my dinner, and such impersonal desires as my desire for a peaceful world. The difference is, he says, that we desire others to share our impersonal desires; we do not always desire others to share our personal desires. He then proceeds to identify moral attitudes with impersonal desires. Consequently he is assuming that one ought to prefer impersonal desires to personal ones. A man who genuinely and consistently furthers his personal desires at the expense of his impersonal ones would, on Russell's view, simply not be acting morally and would be condemned accordingly. Some other philosophers have, I think, made a very similar move with the concept of universalizability. They have defined moral principles as universalizable ones. They have then assumed that anyone who conducts his life by principles which cannot be universalized is just not acting morally and may be condemned accordingly. This is what lies behind Kemp's remark, quoted above, about the egoist.

It is not possible to dispose of the problem of the authority of conscience in this way. A consistent naturalist must say that if, in fact, a man guides his life by maxims of self-interest, and if he does genuinely feel guilt and remorse when he departs from those principles, then, in the naturalist sense of 'ought', he is doing what he thinks he ought to do. He will not be doing what most other people think he ought to do and, as has been argued in the last chapter, that may provide them with quite good grounds for condemning him. One cannot, however, dodge this question by saying that this, or indeed any course of conduct, is ruled out in advance simply by the meaning of the word 'moral'.

PART III

WHAT IS MORALITY?

CHAPTER 12

THE DEFINITION OF MORALITY

According to the naturalist moral reasoning rests, ultimately, on certain axioms which are, when properly understood, not propositions, statements of fact, but expressions of preferences, desires or attitudes. It would be generally agreed, however, that not every preference or desire or attitude is a moral one. Hobbes, indeed, said that 'good' just means 'the object of a desire', without distinguishing between desires. But he then went on to develop what we earlier called a two-level theory of morality. At one level morality consists in those rules which a given society imposes on its members in order to promote peace and security; or, at least, the fundamental ones without which the society would collapse into anarchy. At this level, to say that X ought to be done just means that the doing of X is in accordance with these rules. But we may still ask the further question: Why ought we to try to prevent the society from collapsing? At this level the answer is: Because, without the existence of such a society, you will not be able to gratify any of your desires.

Even for Hobbes, then, while the ultimate moral criterion is simply *a* desire, any desire at all, there are some considerations which have a special title to be called *moral* considerations. Here the criterion is dictated by the end, which is to prevent the society from relapsing into anarchy. Hobbes is mainly concerned with the ultimate rationale of these social rules and does not consider how they appear to the person who obeys them. He has, indeed, been criticized for supposing that every member of society, when he obeys moral rules, has before his mind the need to prevent a relapse into anarchy and the way in which such a relapse would interfere with the gratification of his own desires. It is quite clear that this is not, in fact, the way in which moral rules present themselves to the average citizen.

It is not hard, however, to modify Hobbes's account so as to meet this objection. It is quite in accordance with Hobbes's general view that the society should take care to instil into each member, and especially in the younger generation, a feeling of reverence for the rules of the society and consequent feelings of remorse and guilt, reinforced by punishment of one kind and another, when these rules are broken. This would result in moral rules having a different 'feel' from those personal desires on which, ultimately, they depend. Although they are justified, ultimately, by their function in enabling us to gratify desires, they present themselves, as a result of conditioning in childhood, as ends in themselves, and the remorse and guilt which result from ignoring them feel quite different from the feelings of self-annoyance which we have when we neglect more direct means of gratifying desires. It is natural enough, considering the way in which they are inculcated, that moral rules should present themselves, to use Kant's terminology, as categorical imperatives. This need not prevent them from being, in fact, hypothetical imperatives when we consider not their psychological import to the individual, but their ultimate rationale.

This is the way in which Hobbes's account of morality may be reconciled with that of the other naturalists (or semi-naturalists) who succeeded him and disagreed with him. Butler, Shaftesbury and Hutcheson all regarded the disposition to do one's duty as a distinct part of human nature, quite separate from the tendency to gratify desires. They regarded conscience, or the moral sense, as simply an innate instinctive human tendency to approve of certain kinds of action and to disapprove of other kinds. It was left to Hume to show how these two strands in naturalist theory could be interwoven so as to form a single coherent theory.

It follows from this that morality has two aspects, an internal and an external one, and that one might define it from either of these points of view. A Hobbist might define moral rules as those rules which a given society lays down for its own preservation; but, equally, he might define them as rules which are attended with a quite unique sense of urgency and whose disregard causes quite distinctive feelings of guilt and remorse. The first definition would pay regard to the content of the rules, what specific kind of thing they enjoined or forbade. The second definition would not be concerned with the content, but rather with the kind of attitude with which the moral rule is regarded. In this unusual sense the definition might be called a formal one. Hobbes does, in fact, concern himself with the external aspect of morality. Shaftesbury and Hutcheson, on the other hand, when they ask themselves what morality is, arrive at an answer which is mainly in terms of its internal aspect. They say that morality is a disposition to have certain distinctive feelings of approval and disapproval. Both of them, however, do raise the further question of what is common and peculiar to all the things for which human beings have these feelings. They come up, indeed, with rather different answers. According to Hutcheson, men instinctively approve those actions which are directed towards securing the greatest happiness of the greatest number. According to Shaftesbury, the actions approved by human beings all have a tendency to promote the ultimate purpose of the universe. Neither of them supposes that men are conscious of this, except in a dim and groping way. Each of them would say that morality is a God-given instinct which does in fact have one of these results.

If we now apply to these naturalist theories the remarks about definition made in the last chapter, it will be clear that for all of them 'morality' is a typical term in whose connotation we may find at least two defining characteristics, both of which normally apply to the same thing. It just is a fact that human beings do have certain distinctive attitudes which are directed towards rules with a certain kind of content. 'Morality' is the name which we give to this phenomenon. We might indeed ask ourselves whether we would still use the term 'moral' of the same attitudes if they were directed to a different kind of object, or of the same object if it did not evoke these attitudes. It seems likely that here Hobbes's answer would be different from that of Shaftesbury and Hutcheson. Hobbes would no doubt wish to keep the term 'moral' for the rules necessary for the preservation of society, even if human beings did not feel towards those rules the attitudes which they actually have. Shaftesbury and Hutcheson would no doubt regard as moral any consideration which in fact evoked attitudes of approval. These differences do not, however, affect the essential nature of their moral theories.

Recent moral philosophers in the naturalist tradition have devoted a good deal of attention to the definition of morality. It is possible to divide them into two schools of thought according as they define morality by form or by content. The revolt against objectivism has led some moral philosophers to insist that moral principles are just those which evoke certain attitudes and that different individuals may well have these attitudes towards very different sets of principles. Consequently there has been a tendency to insist that any principle at all could be a moral one. It has been objected to this that there are some principles which we would never concede to be moral ones, however large a part they play in the life of a given individual.

This second view has been urged forcibly by Mrs Philippa Foot. Those who put forward a purely formal definition, she says, are committed to holding

that if we describe a man as being for or against certain actions, bringing them under universal rules, adopting these rules for himself, and thinking himself bound to urge them on others, we shall be able to identify him as holding moral principles, whatever the content of the principle at which he stops. But why should it be supposed that the concept of morality is to be caught in this particular kind of net? The consequences of such an assumption are very hard to stomach; for it follows that a rule which was admitted by those who obeyed it to be completely pointless could yet be recognised as a moral rule. If people happened to insist that no one should run round trees left handed, or look at hedgehogs in the light of the moon, this might count as a basic moral principle about which nothing more need be said.[1]

Mrs Foot's argument is that such principles simply would not count as moral ones, whatever emotions they aroused in the

[1] 'Moral Arguments', *Mind*, LXVII (1958), 512.

person holding them. It is, she suggests, part of the meaning of the word 'moral' that moral rules must have a particular kind of content and not only be the object of a particular kind of attitude. In general, principles which have no connection (or are not believed to have any connection) with human well-being are ruled out. It is not clear whether she would also rule out such injunctions as 'Always cause as much misery as you can'.

Some other philosophers have said that, for example, the egoist's principle ('I shall always further my own interests and ignore other people's') could not be a moral principle, though they have usually said that such a principle is not excluded because of its content but because it lacks some formal feature, such as 'universalizability'.

It seems more plausible, however, to say that trivial principles are excluded by the very meaning of the word 'morality' than to say that selfish or callous ones are. We are presumably trying to define 'moral' in the sense in which the word is contrasted with 'unmoral' or 'non-moral', not in the sense in which it is contrasted with 'immoral'. We are concerned, that is, with the descriptive and not the evaluative use of 'moral'. In saying that some principles are not moral ones, we are not trying to condemn them. We are not ourselves trying to make a moral judgement, but merely to get straight what kind of thing a moral judgement is.

A parallel may be illuminating here. If we say that Bacon's essays are not poetry, but prose, we are not evaluating; but if we say that what Patience Strong writes is not poetry, but verse, or perhaps doggerel, we are evaluating. We are making an aesthetic judgement, which may well be a sound one. As an aesthetic judgement, it needs to be supported by reasons, and the reasons will not be merely linguistic ones. It will not do to say 'We just don't happen to use the word "poetry" of this kind of thing'. This would invite an answer, 'But it may be just as well worth reading, for all that'. If someone were to give us this answer to the statement that Bacon's essays are not poetry, we would say 'That is not in dispute. I didn't mean to imply anything about the literary value of the essays.' But we cannot say that about Patience Strong. For, in this use of 'poetry', to say that something is 'not poetry' *is* to imply something about its literary value. Consequently the remark needs to be supported by an aesthetic theory; it cannot be passed off as a neutral investigation into usage.

In the same way, to say that a given principle is not a moral one may mean that it is immoral, and so to be avoided; or it may mean that it is one about which moral questions just do not arise. If the first, it needs to be backed by reasons which are not merely linguistic reasons. The criterion by which we distinguish between the moral and the immoral will itself be a moral principle, and as such open to attack and defence. The criterion by which we distinguish between the moral and the non-moral, on the other hand, must not itself be a moral principle. An immoral principle is, indeed, a moral one in the other sense of 'moral', that is, it is not non-moral, not outside the sphere of morality. For this reason we may be suspicious of the view that the egoist's principle is not, in this sense, a moral one; for many people would regard it as an immoral principle.

It may be objected that we condemn the egoist, not because he adopts this principle, but because he allows it to usurp the place of moral principles. This objection, however, merely brings out another implication of the word 'moral'. We expect a moral principle to take precedence over others: in the terminology we have been using, it has 'authority'. It can hardly be denied, however, that the egoist's principle has authority *for him*. When it is said that he allows it to usurp the place of a moral principle, what is meant is that he gives it authority when it *ought not* to have authority. It is presupposed that only moral principles ought to have authority. But, if this is so, then to say that a given principle is not a moral one is to say that it is not the kind of principle that ought to take precedence over others. This is clearly not a morally neutral remark.

Indeed, so long as this connotation clings to the word 'moral', it is hard to see how *any* statement to the effect that moral principles are of a particular kind can be morally neutral. Moreover, so long as this connotation clings to the term, it is hard to see how any statement of this kind can be consistent with subjectivism. The subjectivist may of course say that principles of a certain kind do not in fact have authority for anyone. He may also say that he disapproves of principles of a certain kind being given authority. But he cannot consistently say that it is objectively true that principles of a certain kind ought never to be given authority, and that this truth is embodied in the ordinary meaning of the term 'morality'. All that can follow from the definition of moral terms, for him, is that people do in fact treat as authoritative only a certain kind of principle. This would not, however, be consistent with saying that the egoist accords authority to a principle that is not moral.

The point is important, because one suspects that some modern philosophers have used the device of defining morality as a means of softening the rigours of subjectivism. They are unable to accept an objectivist ethic, and feel forced to conclude that moral utterances merely express attitudes that men happen to have acquired. They are, however, reluctant to accept the consequence that they have no reason for condemning the moral attitudes of (say) Hitler except that they do not happen to share them. They try to avoid this conclusion by saying that it applies only to certain kinds of attitude. Others may be excluded simply because, by definition, they are not moral.

It is clear, however, that to say, with Russell, that moral desires are, by definition, those impersonal desires which we want others to share does not excuse us from saying why we think that personal desires should yield to impersonal ones, when they conflict; nor does it justify us in condemning another man if he prefers to give precedence to personal desires. Again, to say, with Hare and several others, that moral principles are, by definition, 'universalizable' does not automatically justify a preference for universalizable principles over ones that cannot be universalized. The hard questions for subjectivism still remain, however morality is defined.

So far, then, my argument has been, first, that any definition of morality should be morally neutral and, secondly, that hardly any definition will be morally neutral in practice, since we naturally interpret the statement that X is not a moral principle to mean that X is not the kind of principle that ought to be given authority. There is a special temptation to interpret it in this way if we would like to exclude certain kinds of principle from consideration but are precluded, by our meta-ethic, from being able to justify their exclusion. Consequently I think that we should be suspicious of any philosopher who tells us that, for example, egoism just does not count as a moral principle.

It may be said, however, that these considerations do not apply to Mrs Foot's contention that utterly trivial principles could not be moral ones. Here there is no danger of confusing what is not immoral with what is not non-moral. 'Don't look at hedgehogs in the light of the moon' is neither moral nor immoral; it is non-moral, outside the sphere of morality al-together. And it is so, not because of any formal features, but because of its content. Nevertheless, when Mrs Foot goes on to argue that it is part of the meaning of 'moral' that moral principles shall be concerned with human well-being there is some danger that we (and she) may assume, perhaps uncon-sciously, that reasons have been given for preferring considera-tions of human well-being to any other considerations that may conflict with them.

The facts to which Mrs Foot calls attention may be very easily understood in the light of the traditional naturalist ana-lysis of morality. On this view, we use the term 'moral' of certain attitudes which human beings do in fact have. There is nothing mysterious about our possession of them. They arise because of the kind of fact that Hobbes points to: the need men have for the co-operation of other men in society, and the dependence of society on our willingness to curb some of our desires. Consequently we are all taught in childhood to attach special importance to certain principles (which may vary, within limits, from society to society and from individual to individual) and to feel emotions of guilt and remorse when we ignore them. All this makes up a social phenomenon of which we are all aware; we need a term to refer to it, and the term happens to be 'morality'. In fact the thing to which we apply the term has a number of different characteristics. It has a certain content; it arouses in us certain characteristic attitudes; we accord it a certain authority. In using the term, we may be thinking of any of these characteristics, or all of them. Quite probably we would find it hard to say, if challenged, which we were thinking of. In this there is no difference between 'morality' and most of the other terms we use. If we are asked whether we would continue to use the same term if we felt the same attitudes towards a different object, or accorded authority to a quite different kind of principle, we are exactly in the position of William James when asked if his companions had gone round the squirrel or of the judge who had to decide in which State the murder took place.

There are, of course, strong arguments either way. We may say, as Mrs Foot does, that we would think it very odd indeed if a man did accord authority to the principle that one must not look at hedgehogs in the light of the moon, unless he believed that human well-being was somehow involved in observing this rule. We may also say, from our knowledge of how moral principles actually develop, that it is, to say the least, highly unlikely that anyone would come to adopt this one. On the other hand, if pressed to consider what is at least a logical possibility, that someone might accord authority to this principle, and feel genuine guilt and remorse if he broke it, we might feel inclined to say that in that unlikely case it would be a genuine moral principle.

The real point here, of course, is that the question 'Could such a principle ever count as a moral one?' is one that calls for a decision. In a sense, it does not matter which way we decide.

What does matter is that we shall not be misled into supposing that the different characteristics all of which cohere in the ordinary connotation of 'morality' are somehow necessarily connected. The connection is synthetic. It is empirically true that we feel the characteristic moral attitudes towards principles with a certain content; and there are very good psychological and sociological reasons why this should be so. Mrs Foot is quite right if her point is that those philosophers who say that anything at all could count as a moral principle are neglecting the social and psychological background that our moral principles actually have. But those philosophers are quite right (in their turn) in insisting that, if, in another universe perhaps, or in very unusual social circumstances, the characteristic moral attitudes and the characteristic moral authority did attach themselves to principles with a very different content, those principles would have the same kind of justification as our own moral attitudes have.

We began this discussion of the definition of morality by saying that naturalists, in maintaining that moral statements express certain attitudes, such as approval, are faced with the question of how these attitudes differ from others. There is no reason why the answer should not be in terms of either their internal or their external characteristics, their form or their content, their 'feel' or their objects. It is important, however, that, if we do include content in our definition, we should not suppose that we have avoided the necessity of answering the question 'Why not guide our lives by principles with a different content?' We have not answered that question by saying that such principles would not be moral, by definition. Similarly, if we include other formal characteristics in our definition besides that of having authority, we still need to answer the question 'Why guide our lives by principles with just these formal characteristics?'

CHAPTER 13

UNIVERSALIZATION

As we have seen, one question that confronts naturalists is: if moral utterances are, ultimately, expressions of certain kinds of attitude, how do these attitudes differ from non-moral ones? So far I have argued that, if any single characteristic is to be singled out as the defining characteristic of moral attitudes, it is that they are over-riding. Otherwise the problem of the authority of conscience becomes insoluble. A very common modern view, however, is that the appropriate defining characteristic is the one which may conveniently, if not very euphoniously, be called universalizability. It will be necessary to examine this contention at some length.

Consider the following sentence forms:

1. If it is   for X it is   for anyone else in the same relevant circumstances.

2. If A is   anything else like A in the relevant respects is   .

The thesis we are to consider is that these statements are analytically true if a moral term is inserted in the blanks. 'Right' is the appropriate moral term for (1), 'good' is the appropriate moral term for (2). It is not maintained that only moral terms will fit these blanks; but it is maintained that all moral terms will fit them. On the other hand, there are some terms such as 'boring' or 'loved' which would not fit them. An interesting example cited by Gellner[1] is a phenomenon much discussed in women's magazines known as love at first sight. Gellner points out that while these magazines frequently discuss the question whether this phenomenon ever in fact occurs, they always assume that the question is an empirical one, whereas, he suggests, there are grounds for supposing that love at first sight is in fact logically impossible. For at a first encounter it is

---

[1] E. A. Gellner, 'Ethics and Logic', Aristotelian Society, *Proceedings*, LV (1954–5), 157–78.

possible to notice only a finite number of characteristics. It would seem to follow, then, that if the man were to meet another girl with precisely the same characteristics, he would feel the same emotion for her. It is, however, part of the definition of love as used in women's magazines that it cannot be felt for more than one person. This conclusion (that love at first sight is logically impossible) can be avoided only by denying that the statement 'he fell in love with Angelina' implies 'he would fall in love with any other girl with the characteristics which he noticed in Angelina'. Whether the emotion called love in the women's magazines actually does exist or not, there can be no doubt that it is at least conceived of as being of this type. In this it contrasts with moral terms.

A similar point is made by G. E. Hughes, who compares the statement 'X is wrong' with the statement 'X rouses indignation in me':

Nor will it do to say that to condemn Smith's action morally is to have or express a certain emotion (say, of indignation) about what he did, or to say words such as, 'Smith ought not to have done that' accompanied by or as an expression of such an emotion. For suppose that half an hour later the conversation turns to the case of Smith once more, and this time I say, 'Smith was quite right to act as he did'; and suppose someone objects, 'But half an hour ago you said he ought not to have done it'; and suppose I reply, 'But half an hour ago I happened to feel indignant, so naturally I said he ought not to have done what he did; now, however, I don't happen to feel indignant any longer, so equally naturally I say he was quite right to do it'— suppose I behave like that, then if the analysis we are considering is correct I shall be said to have been condemning Smith's action morally at time t_1 and exonerating it at time t_2, half an hour later. And, again if the analysis is correct, there will be nothing odd about this, for people commonly do calm down in even less than half an hour. The correct comment, however, if I behave in the way I have described, ought to be that I was not making a *moral* judgment at either time t_1 or time t_2. Certainly a man may *change his mind*, about a moral matter as well as about any other, but it will be comparatively easy to see whether I have changed my mind between time t_1 and time t_2. For one condition which must be fulfilled if I am to be said to have changed my mind is that at time t_2 I must be willing to retract the condemnation of Smith's action which I made at time t_1, and that not merely in the sense that I no longer condemn it now but in the stronger sense that I now admit that I was mistaken in condemning it then. And I shall have to be willing to support my retraction of my condemnation by mentioning features of Smith's action or of its attendant circumstances of which I was previously ignorant, or to which I now attach more weight than I did then, or by referring to moral principles under which I now see Smith's action to be subsumable, and so forth; but not by merely pointing out that I have now cooled down. In the conversation reported above, it is I hope clear that I had not changed my mind at time t_2 (if this is not clear I have reported the conversation badly); my mood had changed, but that is quite a different matter.[1]

The point here is that a moral statement does more than just combine an assertion about my feelings with the further assertion that those feelings were actually roused by certain characteristics of an external object. A moral statement also implies that the same characteristics rouse the same emotions. A distinction is being made between an emotion which is actually roused by a particular combination of characteristics on the one hand and a moral attitude on the other. Putting this in terms of Gellner's example, 'I fell in love with Angelina because she has characteristics p, q, r' does not imply that I feel the same emotion for any other woman with characteristics p, q, r. The statement here is simply that I do have a particular attitude towards Angelina and that that attitude was caused by her characteristics p, q, r. On the other hand, 'Angelina is good because she has characteristics p, q, r' or 'I approve (morally) of Angelina because she has characteristics p, q, r' or 'I condemn (morally) Angelina because she has characteristics p, q, r' all do imply that I have the same attitude towards other women with the same characteristics.

Hughes and the numerous philosophers who agree with him are, then, putting forward the thesis that moral statements have at least the following four characteristics:

1. They are expressions of pro- or anti-attitudes.

2. They refer obliquely to *some* characteristics which cause these attitudes and which are the *objects* of those attitudes. In

---

[1] G. E. Hughes, 'Moral Condemnation', in A. I. Melden (ed.), *Essays in Moral Philosophy* (University of Washington Press, 1958), pp. 108–34.

this, moral statements contrast with such assertions as 'I am feeling miserable', in which, while no doubt it is implied that the emotion has some cause, it is not directed towards any specific object.

3. They imply that the same attitude is felt towards anything else with the same characteristics. Here, as we have seen, the contrast is with such attitudes as love or annoyance.

4. They imply a disposition to encourage other people to have the same attitude towards the same object. Here again moral statements contrast with 'I am in love with Angelina' or 'This always makes me miserable'.

As has already been indicated, this thesis seems to me to be best understood against the background of the traditional naturalist theory. Those who put it forward are as a rule naturalists in the sense that they have been influenced by the kind of arguments put forward by Hutcheson and Hume and by the prevailing metaphysical atmosphere of empiricism to regard moral statements as essentially expressions of pro- or anti-attitudes. Consequently they feel obliged to meet the demand that moral attitudes shall be distinguished from other types of attitude. Moreover, they feel that by making universalizability the distinguishing feature of moral attitudes, they are doing justice to what seems to them the small element of truth in objectivist theories of ethics. Clearly such statements as 'I am feeling miserable' or 'I love Angelina' are subjective in a sense in which 'X is good' or 'I approve of X' are not. This difference, it is felt, can be accounted for without supposing non-natural qualities or any other metaphysically objectionable entities by distinguishing between attitudes which are universalizable and ones which are not.

The view we are considering is summed up with admirable clarity by Hughes in the following sentence:

I am maintaining, then, that whereas the sentence (i) 'whoever condemns X also condemns whatever he regards as similar to X in the relevant respects' expresses a contingent (and incidentally false) proposition, the sentence (ii) 'whoever *morally* condemns X also morally condemns whatever he regards as similar to X in the relevant respects' expresses a logically necessary truth and one that is elucidatory, or at least partially elucidatory, of the meaning of the word 'morally'.

As we have seen, Hughes's contention is that to condemn X is merely to express certain feelings which have been roused by some characteristics of X and which are directed towards X. The feeling in question is not, however, *moral* condemnation unless it is implied that anything else with the same characteristics would rouse the same feelings.

This general thesis, that universalizability is a purely formal, logical feature of moral terms, by which they may be distinguished from most others, was introduced into current philosophical discussion by R. M. Hare, and it is he who has developed it most fully. Hare regards moral utterances as essentially imperatives. What distinguishes them from other (or what Hare calls 'singular') imperatives is just this feature of universalizability. If I say 'Shut the door!' to Jones, I am, in effect, saying 'Let Jones shut the door here and now!' But if I say 'Jones ought to shut the door; it is a standing temptation to thieves to leave it open as he does' I am, in effect, saying 'Let everyone in Jones's circumstances (in this case, perhaps, everyone who leaves empty a room containing valuables) shut the door!'

Moral utterances, then, have two purely formal, and in a sense grammatical, features: they are prescriptive and they are universalizable. This was the main point made in Hare's first book on this subject, *The Language of Morals*. In a second book, *Freedom and Reason*,[1] he applies his thesis in more detail to the problem of distinguishing moral sentiments from others, and in particular from desires and interests. Desires are not universalizable, because 'if I want to do A in these circumstances, I am not committed to wanting anyone else placed in exactly or relevantly similar circumstances to do likewise'.[2] And 'interests likewise are not universalizable; what it is in one person's

---

[1] Oxford, Clarendon Press, 1963.
[2] *Freedom and Reason*, p. 71, §5.4.

interest to have, it is not necessarily in his interest that anyone else should have'.[1]

Hare is consequently able to say, with Kant, that universalizability constitutes a test by means of which we can discover whether a principle on which we propose to act is or is not a moral principle. Let us suppose, for example, that *A* owes money to *B*, who himself owes money to *C*, and that *B* is asking himself whether he ought to have *A* imprisoned for debt. If he decides that he ought, then it follows (as a simple matter of logic) that he himself ought to be imprisoned by *C*. And this in turn entails the singular prescription 'Let *C* imprison *B*'. But this is (as a matter of fact) not acceptable to *B*. Hence, Hare argues, he is compelled to reject the moral judgement '*B* ought to imprison *A*'. This procedure is, Hare contends, precisely parallel to Popper's account of scientific method. 'What knocks out a suggested hypothesis, on Popper's theory, is a singular statement of fact; the hypothesis has the consequence that *p*; but *not-p*.'[2] Similarly, the moral hypothesis has as its consequence a singular prescription, which is (not of course false, but) unacceptable.

There is, of course, the difference that, whereas the scientist cannot make the singular statement of fact true or false, *B* can, if he chooses, accept the consequence and go to prison. To that extent the existentialists are right, and we may choose our own moral principles. The point is that we cannot escape the price of accepting a moral principle. It would make no difference, for example, if *B* had not happened to owe money to *C*. He would still need to search his heart and be quite sure that, if he were ever to contract a debt and be unable to repay it, he would assent to his own imprisonment. The consideration is not, of course, simply a prudential one: 'some day you may be in *A*'s shoes, so you'd better be careful'. Even if *B* is a very rich man who would never be likely to borrow money he must still make the imaginative experiment of supposing himself to be in *A*'s shoes. Sometimes, indeed, it may be empirically im-

[1] *Freedom and Reason*, p. 158, §9.1.   [2] *Ibid.* p. 92, §6.3.

possible for *B* to be in *A*'s shoes: for example, *A* may be a Negro and *B* a white South African. He can still make the imaginative experiment. Only if he is prepared to say sincerely 'But I want to be imprisoned (or whatever) if ever I should be like that' can he be sure that he is acting on a moral principle.

In short, when a man is thinking morally, he is, Hare tells us, 'compelled to universalize his volitions'.[1] The compulsion is a logical one: it is incorrect, or at least eccentric and liable to cause misunderstanding, if words like 'moral' are used to refer to purely personal desires.

To put the matter more plainly: if all that a person is concerned with is how to promote the interests of, *e.g.* his family, let him by all means discuss this question to his heart's content; but let him not confuse this sort of question with that which is troubling the man who asks 'What ought a man (*any* man) to do when faced with circumstances like this?'[2]

Although the point is, to that extent, a verbal one, it is, Hare claims, of great practical use in making moral decisions and in settling moral arguments. For, once we understand the logic of our moral principles, we can test them by asking ourselves whether we are in fact prepared to accept the (hypothetical) consequences of universalizing them. Moreover, Hare claims, we need no longer suppose, as many philosophers do, that 'the only kind of urgent moral argument is one which has as a premiss a moral principle already accepted by both parties to the argument. On the contrary...once the logical character of moral concepts is understood, there can be useful and compelling moral argument even between people who have, before it begins, no substantive moral principles in common.'[3] This is because one disputant can point out to the other the consequences of universalizing the moral premisses he does hold, in the hope of finding one that will be unacceptable to him. That it is unacceptable is a matter of fact: it is not a question of showing that he ought not to accept it (which would require a common moral premise) but simply that he would not be

---

[1] *Ibid.* p. 199, §10.6.   [2] *Ibid.* pp. 165–6, §9.2.
[3] *Ibid.* p. 187, §10.1.

prepared to accept the role of one or other of the people affected by the application of the principle. The difference *may*, of course, be irreconcilable, since there is always a chance that one of the disputants is prepared to accept consequences that the other would not accept: Hare is merely denying that the difference *must* be irreconcilable.

One can see why Hare's position has been regarded as providing a middle way between objectivism and subjectivism. It has been said, indeed, to resolve (or perhaps dissolve) the whole controversy. Once we understand the logic of moral concepts, it is contended, we can see what is sound and what is unsound both in subjectivism and in objectivism. The subjectivist is right in realizing that, ultimately, moral principles are rules of conduct that a man accepts, and that different men may accept different ones; he is wrong in supposing that they are expressions of more or less arbitrary likes and dislikes, and that anything could be a moral principle. The objectivist is right in seeing that a man may be driven to accept moral principles that run counter to his purely personal desires, that they involve both reasoning and rationality, and that some principles could not be treated as moral ones by any sane man; he is wrong in supposing that they express non-empirical truths.

One can see, too, why this view has proved attractive and persuasive. It is now very often accepted as settled that universalizability is a purely formal, logical requirement of morality. Nevertheless, it can, I believe, be shown, and in the following chapters I shall try to show, that this view is a mistaken one, which rests on a confusion.

CHAPTER 14

TYPES OF UNIVERSALIZATION

1. DESCRIPTIVE UNIVERSALIZABILITY

The universalizability thesis may be presented as about moral *terms* or as about moral *principles*. In this chapter it will be considered as a thesis about terms.

Of the two sentence forms mentioned at the beginning of the last chapter, the second would seem to be the relevant one here:

If *A* is   anything else like *A* in the relevant respects is   .

It is a peculiarity of moral predicates, it is suggested, that if you apply one to any one subject you are also, by implication, applying it to anything that is like that subject in the relevant respects. To mention some of Hare's examples, if you say that a picture is good, and I produce another picture exactly like the first (or at least like it in the relevant respects), you cannot deny that it is also good. This still applies even if the picture is in fact unique.

Siamese cats are unique individuals—one is never precisely like another; but this does not mean that judgements made at a cat show about their merits are not universalizable. Even if there were only one Siamese cat in the show, a judge who called it a good one would have to admit that *if* there had been another cat in the show like the first one in all, or in the relevant, respects, the second cat would have been a good one too.[1]

There can be little doubt that this is true: the objection to it is simply that it would seem to apply to any term at all, or almost any. If you say, for example, 'this piece of cloth is yellow', you are certainly implying that another piece like it in the relevant respects is also yellow.

There is indeed one important difference between 'yellow' and 'good'. The 'relevant respect' in which the second piece of cloth is like the first will be simply its yellowness. The other characteristics of the cloth may be quite independent of its

---

[1] *Freedom and Reason*, p. 141, §8.2.

colour. The goodness of something cannot, however, be independent of its other characteristics. If you say that the cloth is good, it is always in order to ask 'What's good about it?' (that is, 'In virtue of what other characteristics is it good?'), and the answer cannot be simply 'Just its goodness'; but one could answer a similar question about 'yellow' by saying 'Just its yellowness'. But to say this is merely to say that 'good' is what Ross calls 'a consequential characteristic', or what Hare calls 'supervenient'. This is, indeed, an important feature of moral terms: some of the most difficult problems about them arise out of the fact that, although something is good by virtue of its good-making characteristics, the assertion that it is good cannot be reduced to the assertion that it has those characteristics. It is generally assumed, however, that universalizability is different from supervenience: that 'good' is both consequential and universalizable. One can concede that 'yellow' is different from 'good' in that it is not consequential; but there does not seem to be any further point of difference that would enable us to say that 'good' is, and 'yellow' is not, universalizable.

What, then, would be an example of a term that is not universalizable? Earlier it was suggested that 'boring' is such a term, and Hughes seems to imply that no terms that merely express emotion are universalizable. There is, however, at least one sense in which this is clearly not true. If I say 'X is annoying' (meaning no more than 'X rouses annoyance in me') I am certainly implying that anything like X in one relevant respect is annoying too: viz. anything like it in rousing annoyance in me. Even if nothing else actually does rouse annoyance in me, I have to concede that, if it did, the term 'annoying' would be applicable to it. The point here is simply that, whatever the meaning-rule for the application of a term, it must apply to everything to which that meaning-rule applies.

This is tautologous, and may seem trivial. But it is in this sense of 'universalizability' that 'yellow' is universalizable. Moreover, it is just because this type of universalizability is clearly a formal, logical requirement of the use of terms that it is important to distinguish it from other types, of which this may not be true. Clearly, if it is only in this sense that moral terms are universalizable, universalizability will not serve to distinguish them from others.

In *Freedom and Reason* Hare recognizes that any descriptive term whatever is universalizable. In one place, indeed, he seems to suggest that value terms are universalizable only because they are descriptive as well as prescriptive: 'The way which I have chosen of explaining what I mean is that the feature of value-judgements which I call universalizability is simply that which they share with descriptive judgements; namely the fact that they both carry descriptive meaning.'[1]

What sort of terms, then, are not universalizable? Hare's own candidate would seem to be what he calls 'singular imperatives'. The peculiarity of moral terms, he tells us, is that they are both prescriptive and universalizable, whereas descriptive terms are universalizable without being prescriptive. The contrast, then, is with those terms which are like moral terms in being prescriptive but unlike them in being singular, rather than universal, prescriptions. And indeed Hare does tell us that singular imperatives are not universalizable. It seems clear, however, that, so far as he is talking about the kind of universalizability that descriptive terms have, this is a mistake. For, according to Hare, both prescriptive and indicative utterances have two elements, which he calls the phrastic and the neustic. The command 'Shut the door!' can, he tells us, be rendered as

Your shutting the door in the immediate future, please,

and the assertion 'You are going to shut the door' as

Your shutting the door in the immediate future, yes![2]

Now the phrastic element which both have in common, 'Your shutting the door in the immediate future', is a descriptive phrase. If I say of a given state of affairs that it is an instance of your shutting the door, I am certainly committed to saying that

---

[1] *Freedom and Reason*, p. 15, §2.4.
[2] *The Language of Morals* (Oxford, Clarendon Press, 1952), pp. 17–18, §2.1.

another state of affairs like the first in the relevant respects is also such an instance. It follows that singular imperatives do have a descriptive element and do have descriptive universalizability.

In one place Hare does seem to recognize this. 'All words which are evaluative', he tells us, 'are also prescriptive; but there are expressions which are prescriptive but not evaluative (because they do not carry descriptive meaning as well). The ordinary singular imperative—*or rather, to be strictly accurate, its "neustic"*—is of this kind.'[1]

This is an astonishing statement, because the neustic ('please') is presumably common to all prescriptive utterances, whether evaluative or not. Moreover, since the whole point of the distinction between the phrastic and the neustic is to separate what is asserted or commanded (which might be thought of as the descriptive element) from the asserting or commanding, it would seem that the neustic element in any sentence is not descriptive. Even this may indeed be doubted, since if anything counts as an instance of asserting or commanding, anything like it in the relevant respects must also be such an instance. There is a sense then in which even the neustic element in sentences, whether or not it makes sense to call such an element descriptive, has the kind of universalizability that attaches to descriptions.

However this may be, it is quite clear that Hare is quite wrong, both in denying descriptive meaning (and so universalizability) to singular imperatives as a whole, and in asserting that it is this absence of descriptive meaning that distinguishes non-evaluative from evaluative prescriptions. He has not established that there are expressions (as distinct from 'elements' in such expressions) that are prescriptive but 'do not carry descriptive meaning as well', and if there are indeed elements in expressions of which this is true, these elements are clearly common to both evaluative and non-evaluative prescriptions (and indeed to non-prescriptive utterances also, since 'yes'

---

[1] *Freedom and Reason*, p. 27, §2.8. My italics.

would not seem to be different from 'please' in this respect).
Singular imperatives, then, are not the non-universalizable
terms we are looking for. Indeed, the only terms that lack
descriptive universalizability would seem to be proper names,
and what Russell called 'logically proper names'—demonstratives like 'this', 'that', 'here' and 'there'.

2. CONSEQUENTIAL UNIVERSALIZABILITY

In spite of the distinction that can be made between descriptive
and emotive meaning, terms whose function it is to express
emotion do have descriptive universalizability, as has been
shown above. It will, nevertheless, be useful to consider more
fully the claim that such terms lack universalizability, because
this may bring to light a rather different type of universalizability.

The terms being considered are those that Nowell-Smith
calls *A*-words: 'words that indicate that an object has some
properties which are apt to arouse a certain emotion or range
of emotions'.[1]

Hughes, it will be remembered, distinguishes between 'condemns' and 'morally condemns', saying that the sentence
'whoever condemns *X* also condemns whatever he regards
as similar to *X* in the relevant respects' is contingent (and
actually false), whereas the corresponding statement about
'morally condemns' is necessarily true. His point is simply
that what bores or annoys you on a given occasion may not
bore or annoy you on another occasion, when you are more
alert or less irritable. To admit this is not, however, to
retract the judgement made on the first occasion; whereas to
admit that you no longer feel moral disapproval for something
is to retract your first judgement. 'I thought it right then, but
I do not think it right now' is perfectly intelligible; 'it was
right then but it is not right now, though nothing has changed
in the meantime but my feelings about it' is not intelligible. On

[1] P. H. Nowell-Smith, *Ethics* (Harmondsworth, Penguin Books, 1954), p. 72.

the other hand 'it was boring (or annoying) then, but it is not now, though nothing has changed in the meantime but my feelings about it' is perfectly intelligible.

But is this true? Would not we be at least equally inclined to say: 'I was annoyed (bored) by it at the time, but I see now that it is not annoying (boring) after all'? Alternatively we might say 'It is undoubtedly annoying (boring) but somehow I was not annoyed (bored) by it that evening'. Sometimes, indeed, we may say 'His speech was boring', meaning no more than that the audience was in fact bored by it; but more commonly to say that X is boring is to say, as Nowell-Smith puts it, that X has those characteristics that are *apt* to bore (either people generally, or the person making the judgement). The phrase 'apt to...' is, it must be admitted, itself ambiguous: it may mean either 'worthy of...', 'what *ought* to rouse...' or 'what *usually* rouses...'. Words like 'boring' may be used in either way: we may say either 'Most people are bored by it, not because it's boring but because they are too lazy mentally to try to understand it' or 'Admittedly it's boring, but only because most people are too lazy mentally to try to understand it'.

It is clear that to say that something is 'apt to bore' (or whatever) in either of these senses is to imply that anything else with the same relevant characteristics is also apt to bore. Only if 'it was boring' is used to mean 'it did actually bore me' (on a given occasion) can we avoid this implication. And now it becomes doubtful whether moral terms are different in this respect. Hughes contrasts 'condemns' with 'morally condemns'. But if I condemn X morally on a given occasion and later withdraw my condemnation, I do not of course withdraw the assertion that I did in fact condemn X on that occasion.

Let us suppose that a father is annoyed by his small daughter, who rushes into his room when he happens to be in a bad mood. He says, to himself, 'Annoying child!' and to his daughter 'You are a naughty girl'. Later, when he has calmed down (having now had his morning coffee), he makes amends to the child and withdraws his condemnation. 'Daddy didn't really mean that you were naughty; you weren't naughty at all.' Does he also withdraw the assertion that she was 'annoying'? In the more usual senses of the word, I think he does. 'There was nothing annoying in what she did; it was just that I was in a bad mood.'

It may be argued, however, that, in saying that the child's behaviour was not annoying, the father does not deny that the emotion he felt was annoyance. In retracting the statement that she was naughty, however, he is saying that the emotion he felt was not *moral* disapproval. To that extent this example supports the contention that moral utterances are more than mere expressions of a particular kind of emotion. To call an emotion a moral one, it is suggested, is not just to say something about the feeling-tone of the emotion. It is, however, misleading to put this by saying that moral terms are universalizable whereas terms expressing emotions are not. For whenever we express our emotions not merely by grunts, groans or smiles but by projecting them on to the objects that evoke them ('X is annoying', 'X is amusing', etc.), we do imply that the same emotion will be roused by similar objects.

It is I think clear that what is at issue here is not descriptive universalizability, but something rather different. It has to do with another feature of moral terms, which Hare seems inclined to confuse with descriptive universalizability: their 'supervenient' or 'consequential' character. A-terms, too, are consequential. If I say that something is annoying, or boring, it does make sense to ask 'What's annoying (boring) about it?' Terms denoting consequential characteristics may be universalizable in two quite different ways. To say 'X is annoying' is to imply, not merely that anything that, like X, has the relational characteristic of rousing annoyance in me is also annoying (descriptive universalizability), but also that anything which has the other characteristics which give rise to that relational characteristic is also annoying. We may call this second way in which terms are universalizable 'consequential universalizability'.

It is clearly consequential, and not descriptive, universalizability that Bernard Mayo has in mind when he contrasts 'a good spade' with one that has merely sentimental value. Mayo tells us that, if someone says 'This is a good spade', he is not just saying that he prefers it to most others. He is also saying, or at least implying, that he would prefer any other spade with the same relevant characteristics to spades without them. On the other hand, he says, if someone tells you that he prefers this spade to most others for sentimental reasons, you are not entitled to draw this inference.[1]

But is this true? After all, there must be something about the sentimentally valued spade that rouses this attitude in the speaker. It may be, for example, that this is the spade with which his late wife used to dig the garden on sunny week-ends while he watched her from a deck-chair in the shade. You are certainly entitled to infer that the spade has *some* characteristic of this sort, some connection with his personal history, and so some one of a wide but fairly definite range of characteristics. And this is all you are entitled to infer about the good spade. Moreover, you are certainly entitled to infer that he will have the same feelings for other spades with the same *relevant* characteristics. If his wife had two spades, for example, which she used on alternate week-ends, and there is no relevant difference between them, he will presumably cherish the other spade as well.

There is, it is true, an important difference between good spades and sentimentally valued ones; but it is not the difference that Mayo specifies. What the difference does consist in is just this: the 'relevant respects' in which one sentimentally valued spade must be like another are different from those in which one good spade must be like another. It might even be said that they are not characteristics of the spade at all: it is just that the spade has played a particular part in the speaker's personal history. More accurately, the characteristics are not intrinsic,

---

[1] B. Mayo, *Ethics and the Moral Life* (London, Macmillan, 1958), pp. 24–6.

but relational. The distinction between intrinsic and relational characteristics is, indeed, an important one, and of great relevance to the whole question of what kinds of judgement we are prepared to call moral ones; but it ought not to be confused with universalizability, whether descriptive or consequential.

Gellner's example is more successful. Edwin's love for Angelina is evoked by qualities which he detects in her; but it does not follow (nor is he implying when he says 'I love you for your...') that the next time he detects these qualities in a girl he will fall in love with her too. There is of course a perfectly intelligible reason for this inconsistency: his affections are already engaged. The relevant circumstances, that is to say, are not the same. The difference, however, is in the person who feels the emotion, not in the object which evokes it. One might, indeed, say that here, as with 'sentimentally valued', the intrinsic characteristics are the same but the relational characteristics are not. What Angelina has got that the other girl has not is the relational characteristic of having-met-Edwin-when-his-affections-were-not-engaged.

There is, all the same, an important difference between the two. When you attach sentimental value to something, you are well aware that you do so because it has played a particular part in your personal history: this relational characteristic is your reason for valuing it. Moreover, this is implied in the use of the phrase 'sentimental value'. Edwin's fancy-free condition is not, however, one of *his* reasons for falling in love, though it may be one of *the* reasons.

When someone has an attitude to something, there are two variables involved: the qualities of the object and the predisposition of the person. If a different object does not rouse the same attitude, it may be because its qualities differ; but it may also be that it has the same qualities, and that it is the person who has changed. We may say that a term has consequential universalizability (or is consequentially universalizable) if only a change in the first of these variables (the qualities of the object) would render it inapplicable.

As we have seen, *A*-words are consequentially universalizable, since to say 'O is annoying' is different from saying 'O annoys me'. Terms like 'sentimentally valued' also have consequential universalizability: or at least they are not precluded from having it by the fact that the qualities of the object implicitly referred to are relational ones. (A man may of course have a change of mood, perhaps brought about by mere lapse of time, as a result of which he ceases to attach sentimental value to something, but that is a different point.) Expressions like '*X* is annoyed by' or '*X* is bored by', referring to a particular occasion, may be said to lack consequential universalizability so far as they do not imply that *X* will be bored or annoyed by the same kind of thing on a different occasion. '*X* is bored by *o* at time *t*' does imply that *X* would be bored at time *t* by other things like *o* in the relevant respects, though not necessarily at time *t*₁. On the other hand '*X* is in love with *Y* at time *t*' does not imply that *X* is in love, even at time *t*, with everyone like *Y* in the relevant respects.

3. SOCIAL UNIVERSALIZABILITY

If it is   for *X* it is   for anyone else in the same relevant circumstances.

This is clearly a different claim from the one we have been considering. So far the question has simply been whether, if something is boring, or yellow, or good, or loved, something else with similar relevant characteristics is necessarily boring, or yellow, or good, or loved. We have not asked whether, if something is boring, or good, or yellow to you, or loved by you, it is necessarily boring or good or yellow to everyone else, or loved by everyone else, in the same relevant circumstances.

This kind of universalization is more often applied to principles than to terms, and will concern us in the next chapter; but it is not wholly inapplicable to terms. Mayo, for example, tells us that the assertion '*X* is a good spade' not only entitles us to infer that the speaker would prefer any other spade with the same relevant characteristics to one without them; but also that any other competent gardener would have the same preference.

The term 'universalizability' is used to refer to a claim of this kind quite as often as it is used in the senses already distinguished. Many writers, indeed, use 'universalizable' to refer to any term that fits either of the sentence forms given at the beginning of the last chapter, without distinguishing between them. It is, however, advisable to make the distinction; and in order to do so I shall use the term 'social universalizability' (or 'socially universalizable').

It may be argued that any term whatsoever is socially universalizable. Take 'yellow', for example. If I say that X is yellow, I am certainly implying that anyone else with normal eyesight will also judge it to be yellow. Nor is this merely a peculiarity of terms denoting secondary qualities: if I say 'X is square' I am implying that other competent judges will call it square.

Social universalizability, in short, is, like descriptive universalizability, a necessary feature of the application of meaning-rules. Not only must a meaning-rule which applies in a given situation also apply in any relevantly similar situation (this is what is meant by calling it a rule), but when one speaker applies it in a given situation he must presuppose that others will apply it in the same way in the same situation. Otherwise he would not be understood. This is simply a consequence of language being a social activity: it is part of what is meant when it is said that a private language is logically impossible.

This is not, however, what is meant when it is claimed that, for example, something that is boring to me may not be boring to someone else in the same circumstances. For it is not denied that if I find it unpleasant to take any interest in someone's conversation, and feel a strong urge to stop paying attention to it, and someone else also finds it unpleasant to take any interest in this conversation, and also feels a strong urge to stop paying attention to it, both he and I will find it boring. 'The relevant circumstances' here are not just those circumstances which would be specified by a rule for the use of the word 'boring'.

Unless, indeed, such a rule specified the 'boredom-making characteristics' that are implicitly referred to. For it is 'boring' as a consequential characteristic that we are here concerned with. The features of a speech, conversation, or occasion that make it boring are fairly definite: the repetition of much that is familiar, or, alternatively, unintelligible, the absence of anything that touches on one's central interests, and so on. These are, of course, relational characteristics: what is familiar or unintelligible to one man will not be so to another; my central interests may be very different from yours. Even so, someone who said that he found his trial for murder (or his first love affair) boring would be making a paradoxical remark, much as if he said that Gandhi was a bad man and Hitler a good one.

To say that a term has consequential universalizability is to say that, when I apply a consequential term X, I imply that the term is applicable to anything else with relevantly similar 'X-making' characteristics, whether intrinsic or relational. To say that a consequential term also has social universalizability (as a consequential, and not merely as a descriptive, term) is to say that, when I apply a consequential term, X, I am implying that other people would also apply the term to anything with relevantly similar 'X-making' characteristics, whether intrinsic or relational.

Mayo tells us that, when we talk of good spades, we are making implicit reference to a consensus of opinion: not about the meaning of the word 'good' (that it is a term of commendation, implies praise, approval, etc.) but about the standards which we apply in appraising the objects of our commendation, praise or approval. He is saying, in fact, that 'good' is socially universalizable.

It is doubtful, however, whether he is right in suggesting that the term 'sentimentally valued' is not. For, when you say that the spade has sentimental value for you, you are certainly

implying that other people will value spades with the same
relevant characteristics (the relational characteristic of having
played a particularly intimate part in one's personal history).

The man who values the spade belonging to his late wife, for
example, implies that other sentimental widowers will value
their wives' possessions, just as the man who talks about a good
spade is implying that other competent gardeners would choose
this spade too. It is true that to talk about 'other sentimental
widowers' is not quite like talking about 'other competent
gardeners'. The first phrase refers to other people with the
same feelings as you have; the second to other people with
the same purposes as you have. Now, if you say something
about your feelings, of course you imply something about
other people with the same feelings. This comes very close to
being a tautology. It is not quite a tautology: for you are implying that there *are* other people with the same feelings. If
that were not the case, if sentimentality were a phenomenon
peculiar to you, you would not be understood. Moreover, to
talk about feelings of this kind is not merely to talk about a
particular kind of sensation. To say that something is sentimentally valued is to say, not merely that it has the relational
characteristic of evoking a particular sensation, but also that it
has the further relational characteristic of being intimately
associated with your personal history. We discriminate between feelings far more by means of the characteristics (including relational characteristics) which evoke them, than by
means of a 'phenomenological' analysis of their 'feeling-tone'.
Consequently, *A*-terms are socially universalizable. The claim
that they are not turns out to turn on the distinction between
relational and intrinsic characteristics. It is, however, misleading to say that a term is not universalizable when all that is
meant is that the characteristics to which implicit reference is
made are relational rather than intrinsic.

It may perhaps be objected that there is a difference between
saying that anyone else in the same circumstances would make
the same judgement as oneself and the claim that in judging for

oneself one is *ipso facto* judging for others as well. At least with
A-words, however, the distinction does not denote any real
difference. If you say that *X* would find something boring, you
are saying that it is boring for him. Does this, however, apply
to 'right'? For, while it does not make sense to say 'This is
boring for *X*, whether he thinks it boring or not', it does make
sense to say 'This is right for *X*, whether he thinks it right or
not'. This distinction will need to be discussed more fully later.
At the moment we may notice that there is at least a superficial
plausibility in the view that, when it is said that 'if something is
right for *X*, it is right for others in the same circumstances', it
is social universalizability that is being referred to. Certainly
this seems to be what Mayo has in mind when he says that
moral terms presuppose a consensus of opinion about standards.
It also seems to be what Hume means when he says that in
moral judgements we adopt the standpoint of an impartial
observer in order to make communication possible.

So far we have been considering universalizability as a feature
of terms, that is, as an essential part of the meaning of some
words. It will be convenient to summarize our conclusions:

1. All words, except proper names and demonstratives, are
descriptively universalizable: that is, they apply to whatever has
the characteristics to which they refer. This is, of course, a
tautology. Proper names and demonstratives are exceptions
only because their function is to pick out an individual as an
individual, and so to distinguish it from other individuals with
similar characteristics.

2. Similarly, all descriptively universalizable words are also
socially universalizable: that is, it is presupposed that other
speakers of the language will use the word in the same way.
This is a necessary consequence of the fact that words are used
to communicate.

3. Some words have a double reference: they refer primarily
to one characteristic or set of characteristics (which may be the
relational characteristic of being the object of a feeling or some
other mental state) and secondarily to some other character-

istic or set of characteristics which give rise to the first. Such words necessarily have descriptive universalizability in respect of the primary reference: they may, and usually do, have *consequential universalizability* in respect of the secondary reference.

4. Such words may, and usually do, have *social universalizability* in respect of the secondary reference.

CHAPTER 15

THE UNIVERSALIZABILITY OF RULES AND PRINCIPLES

1. RANDOM AND ARBITRARY ACTIONS

Hare, in *The Language of Morals*, contrasts 'ought' with other imperatives. The difference, he tells us, is just this: that 'ought' is universalizable while these other ('singular') imperatives are not. 'Use the starting-handle', he tells us, is a prescription which 'applies directly only to the occasion on which it is offered'. On the other hand, 'you ought to use the starting-handle', though it too applies directly to an individual occasion, 'also invokes or appeals to some more general... prescription', such as 'If the engine fails to start at once on the self-starter, one ought always to use the starting-handle'.[1]

What this amounts to is that ought-sentences are, and singular imperatives are not, backed by reasons, and that it is characteristic of reasons that, if they apply to this occasion, they apply to all relevantly similar occasions.

This is undoubtedly true. Suppose (to take another example) that at a party you reject one glass of beer and choose another, giving as your reason that the first glass of beer was flat. We are certainly entitled to infer that on another occasion (perhaps at another party) you will regard the flatness of a glass of beer as a reason for rejecting it. It is true that you may not always act on that reason: at a party, for example, at which you do not know your host so well and are afraid that rejecting a glass of beer may seem rude. Here the relevant circumstances are not the same. Or if we like we can say, perhaps more accurately, that the relevant circumstances (the flatness of the beer and your own taste) are the same; that you have, therefore, a reason for rejecting the beer, but that you also have a reason (and a stronger one) for not rejecting it.

[1] P. 156, §10.3.

170

Suppose, however, that, having given the flatness of the beer as your reason for rejecting it at the first party, you deliberately choose a glass of flat beer at the second party, at the same time assuring us that you have no countervailing reasons and that your taste in beer has not changed in the meantime. 'The flatness of *that* glass of beer', you tell us, 'was a reason for rejecting it: the flatness of *this* glass of beer is not a reason for rejecting it. There is no other relevant difference between the two glasses, or in the surrounding circumstances.' We would be at a loss to understand you, and would have to conclude that your use of the word 'reason' was not the same as ours.

To say that something is a reason for your action on a given occasion, then, is clearly to imply that it will also be a reason for a similar action on another relevantly similar occasion. The word 'reason' is, in short, consequentially universalizable.

Hare's point would seem to depend on this. According to him the use of 'ought' implies a command backed by a reason. It may be argued, however, that this is true of singular imperatives in just the same way as it is true of ought-sentences. Hare's claim is a very cautious one: he says merely that, in uttering ought-sentences, 'we seem to imply (in a loose sense) that there is *some* principle...that we are invoking—though it may not be at once clear, even to us, what the principle is'.

This much is certainly true, at least as a general rule, of singular imperatives. If your instructor tells you to use the starting-handle, it is certainly reasonable to object: 'But yesterday, in precisely the same situation, you told me (or your other pupil) not to use the starting-handle.' And you can say this whether he said 'Use the starting-handle!' or 'You ought to use the starting-handle'. It makes no difference: for, in either case, you are entitled to assume that his instructions are not arbitrary ones.

Hare admits this; but his point is that, if the instruction *were* arbitrary, it would still be couched in the imperative; whereas it could not be put in the form of an ought-sentence: this would be 'logically illegitimate' and 'so eccentric' a use of the word 'ought' as 'to make people wonder what I meant by it'.

If Hare is right, then 'You ought to use the starting-handle; but there is no particular reason; you just ought to use it' would be self-contradictory whereas 'Use the starting-handle; there is no particular reason; just use it' would not be. This may be true; but it hardly seems obviously true. Both sentences seem odd (or 'logically illegitimate') in precisely the same way, and cause just the same kind of bewilderment. Hare's own example does not help much. The instructor may, he suggests, 'be merely prescribing for this particular occasion (perhaps because [he has] thought "Let's see if he knows how to crank a car") without any thought of there being a general principle for all occasions of this kind'. But: (i) In that case, there *is* an appeal to a general principle ('when there is doubt about whether one can exercise a skill, one ought to try to exercise it'; or perhaps, 'the way to perfect one's use of the starting-handle is just to use it'). (ii) In this situation, the instructor might well say 'You ought to use the starting-handle now, so that we can see how well you can do that'.

Let us, however, concede this point to Hare. Perhaps it is true that some commands are arbitrary, and that these can be expressed by the singular imperative, but not by the use of 'ought'. Even if true, however, this is quite misleading. It is misleading because it suggests that here we have an essential difference between singular imperatives on the one hand and ought-sentences on the other. The truth is that this is a difference between all ought-sentences, plus nearly all singular imperatives, on the one hand, and a few very rare, quite unimportant, quite uncharacteristic imperatives on the other. It is clear that this will not tell us very much about what marks ought-sentences off from all other types of sentence, whether the 'ought' in question is the moral or the non-moral 'ought'.

The difference Hare points to probably arises from the fact that the imperative form is characteristically used to give orders or instructions, while 'ought' is characteristically used to give advice or admonitions. If someone gives an order what is (loosely) implied is not that there is no reason or principle behind the order, but that it is not for the recipient of the order to concern himself with the reason. If the sergeant-major shouts 'Attention!' it is not for the private to ask why, and if he does ask the answer will be (in effect, at any rate) 'because I tell you to'. But, if the colonel asks 'Why did you stand the men to attention?' the sergeant-major will find it necessary to give a reason, and not only to give a reason but to invoke one of Hare's 'type *B* principles' ('One ought always to call troops to attention when...'). In the order-giving situation it is the man who gives the order who takes the responsibility for the action. That is why the reason for the action need not concern the agent. But, if you accept advice, the responsibility for the action is still yours, and the principle behind it does concern you. To accept advice, then, is to accept the principle behind the advice; but to carry out an order is not necessarily to accept the principle behind it. This comes out clearly when a subordinate asks his superior 'Is that an order, sir?', implying that he disapproves of the action and will not do it unless ordered to. He does not accept the principle behind the action; consequently he will not do it if he has merely been advised, and not ordered, to do it.

While it is, then, misleading to say, without qualification, that singular imperatives are not universalizable, we do have here certain types of utterance which may be said, in one sense, to lack universalizability: arbitrary commands, or statements about random or whimsical actions. Other commands or statements about action imply (loosely) that there is a reason for them, and consequently that similar commands would be given or actions done in relevantly similar circumstances.

2. RULES OF THUMB

Since the word 'reason' is (consequentially) universalizable, it is possible to extract a rule or principle from any statement that an action is done for a reason. That is why Kant was able to claim that any action has a 'maxim'. Is the converse true? Is it possible to state a rule for acting without specifying the reason for the action?

At first sight, one is inclined to say that it is, since we distinguish between 'rules of thumb' and other rules precisely because those who apply rules of thumb do not know the reasons for them. We come up here, however, against the ambiguity of the concept of having a reason. Consider the neurotic or the child who scrupulously treads only on every third paving stone, going to great pains to avoid the others. This is, in a sense, an action for which no reason can be given. Of course a psychoanalyst might discover one; but there is no conscious reason, no answer which the agent can give if we ask him 'Why do you tread only on every third stone?' On the other hand, if we ask him instead 'Why do you tread on this stone rather than that?' he has a reason, 'Because it is the third.' Reasons of this sort can also be given for rules of thumb. Without them, indeed, one would not have a rule at all. Since a rule must be applicable to other situations besides the one in which we find ourselves, there must be some feature by which we can recognize such situations.

Rule-universalizability of this type is the counterpart of the descriptive universalizability that terms have. Indeed, it is the genus of which descriptive universalizability is one species. We acknowledge this when we speak of meaning-rules. We cannot apply a term at all unless there is some feature of the situation which tells us when to apply it.

Since we must be able to recognize other situations to which they apply, rules have at least one formal feature: it must be possible to express them in a sentence that does not contain any 'egocentric particulars': that is, words like 'this', 'here' and 'now'. Suppose the foreman says to the apprentice 'Pull this lever; now press that button; now push the rod nearest you'. If these instructions are to be useful to the apprentice when he operates another machine, or even when he operates this machine on another occasion, he will need to replace 'this', 'that', 'now' and 'you' by other terms. For example: 'Pull the large, black lever; after five seconds or so press the topmost button; after another five seconds push the rod nearest the operator.'

This translation gives us the instruction in a form in which it is generally applicable. But it is still only a rule of thumb. Can it be said to give us the reason, or principle, behind the instruction? Clearly, it cannot. It is quite possible that, on another machine, the corresponding lever will be red, not black; the corresponding button at the bottom, not the top; the corresponding rod farthest from the operator, and not nearest to him. This does not mean, however, that the translated instruction could not apply to the other machine, for that machine might well have another black lever, and there will have to be another button which is the topmost one, and another rod which is the nearest one. What it does mean is that, when he does apply the translated instruction, the apprentice will not get the results he wants; nor will he be acting on the principle on which the foreman acts. That principle would presumably be 'Pull the lever which operates the such-and-such' (and so on).

What this brings out is that there is a difference between a rule of general application and a rule which reveals the underlying reason or principle. In order to get either, we need to eliminate egocentric particulars and replace them with descriptive phrases; but a descriptive phrase may give us a rule of general application (and so perhaps *a* principle) without giving us *the* principle or *the* reason behind the rule: without giving us, in Kant's words, the 'maxim' of the action.

This distinction is closely parallel to the one between the descriptive and the consequential universalizability of terms. 'Pull the black lever' gives the apprentice a rule to apply, but does not succeed in specifying the characteristic of the lever that makes it advisable to pull it. It is not because it is black that the lever is to be pulled, but because it operates the such-and-such. We cannot infer 'In relevantly similar circumstances (for example, on other machines), pull any black lever' but we can infer 'In relevantly similar circumstances, pull any lever that operates the such-and-such'. Similarly, if you say 'His smugness is irritating' you do imply that it is because he is smug that he is irritating, and that in relevantly similar circumstances other people's smugness will also be irritating.

3. SOCIAL UNIVERSALIZABILITY AND RULES

Is there also a parallel to social universalizability? At first sight it might seem that there must be. For we have said that one kind of social universalizability is necessarily connected with descriptive universalizability and that descriptive universalizability attaches to meaning-rules by virtue of their being rules. Nevertheless, it does not follow that all rules have this kind of social universalizability. For there can be private rules in the sense in which there cannot be private languages. I may make it a rule always to step only on the third paving stone without either telling others about this rule or expecting them to share it. If meaning-rules have descriptive universalizability by virtue of being rules, they have social universalizability by virtue of being about meaning; for it is as a result of social conventions that words have meaning.

The case is different with the kind of social universalizability that is connected with consequential universalizability. For, if I have a reason for stepping on the third paving stone (to win a bet, say), it will be a reason for anyone else in relevantly similar circumstances.

A rule that succeeds in stating the 'maxim' of an action, that is to say, will be a rule for anyone else in relevantly similar circumstances. This results from the implications of words like 'reason'. If R is a reason for X to do Q, it is (i) a reason for X to do something like Q in similar circumstances; (ii) a reason for someone else, Y, who is like X in the relevant respects, to do something like Q in similar circumstances. If we reserve the term 'principles' for those rules that succeed in revealing the reasons underlying them, we may say that principles are consequentially universalizable as a result of (i) and socially universalizable as a result of (ii).

Universalizability of Rules and Principles

Is there not, however, a difference between saying that a principle is generally accepted and saying that, in laying down a principle for oneself, one is necessarily laying it down for others too? Suppose that *X* is an examiner who makes it a principle never to give *A*s to a candidate unless he shows originality as well as knowledge. *Y* disagrees with him: undergraduates, he argues, should not be expected to do original work under examination conditions. What is a principle for *X* is not a principle for *Y*. Nevertheless, it may still be said that *X*'s principle applies to anyone who is like him in the relevant respects: not simply in being an examiner, but in being an examiner who shares his views about the purpose of examinations.

Now, it was suggested that *A*-words are socially universalizable in the sense that, in using them, we abstract from individual peculiarities. We call things 'boring' or 'irritating' if we think that most people would find them so: if we are aware that we are different from other people, we can quite well say 'It bores me, though it's not really boring'. It is clear, however, that even 'it bores me' does imply that it will also bore anyone else who is like me in the relevant respects. This may seem empty enough, since the only similarity that we are able to specify may be that he too is bored by this sort of thing. Nevertheless, the point is important. For boredom is not an isolated phenomenon: it has an explanation, and it is the nature of explanations to have application beyond a single individual.

I may not, of course, know what the explanation of my boredom is. Even if I do know (for example, that it is due to my being tone-deaf, or untrained in art, or ignorant of mathematics) I will still be bored whether or not I am aware of the explanation. To act on a principle, on the other hand, is to have a reason for acting of which we are aware, and which would not influence us if we were not aware of it. Nevertheless, such reasons are universalizable only in the way that explanations are: they will be reasons for anyone who is like me in the relevant respects, which may include all sorts of idiosyncrasies.

Even if I am unique, the sole member of a one-member class, my reasons are still universalizable in the sense that, if there were any other members of this class, they too would have a similar reason for acting. If my reason is to win a bet, for example, the fact that no one else has made this bet does not prevent my reason from being universalizable in the sense we are considering.

So far, then, it has been said that all rules must be capable of general application, and consequently of being stated without the use of egocentric particulars; that, in addition, principles—rules which are more than rules of thumb and reveal the reasons behind them—have both consequential and social universalizability. That is to say, the reasons will apply to the same agent in relevantly similar circumstances, and to other agents who are like this one in the relevant respects. These respects, however, may include relational as well as intrinsic characteristics.

What, then, has been meant by those who claim that universalizability is somehow peculiar to, or at least especially characteristic of, *moral* principles? Non-moral principles, it is implied, may well be non-universalizable. But how can they be, if universalizability is, as I have been maintaining, a necessary feature of principles as such, whether moral or non-moral?

We may best answer these questions by considering some of the kinds of principle that are often alleged to be non-universalizable.

Consider, for example, this principle:

(P) Let me do whatever will make my country triumph over all others.

If this is to be universalized, the personal pronouns must obviously be eliminated. If the principle is to apply generally, the first pronoun may become 'everyone': 'Let everyone do whatever...' But how are we to translate the 'my'? Is it to be
(P 1) 'Let everyone do whatever will make his country triumph over all others'? If so, we have merely replaced a pronoun in the first person with one in the third person. And this is at

least like an egocentric particular in that the phrase 'his country' may change its reference when the rule is applied by different people. An Englishman who tries to follow this principle will do what he can to make England triumph over all other countries: an Australian will do what he can to make Australia triumph over all other countries, and so on.

The elimination of egocentric particulars is necessary simply to enable a rule to be applied at all in a different situation. It cannot be said, however, that P 1 is impossible to apply. We know quite well what kind of conduct it would lead to. But perhaps it is impossible for *everyone* to apply it, both the Englishman and the Australian? For clearly it is not possible for England to triumph over all other countries, including Australia, and for Australia at the same time to triumph over all other countries, including England. P 1 then, it may be argued, involves a contradiction. Such principles, then, cannot be universalized.

This is, however, false. It is, of course, impossible for everyone to succeed in making his country triumph over all others; but it is quite possible for everyone to try. But, it will be objected, isn't it pointless, and so irrational, to try to do something when success has been ruled out in advance? The answer is that it is neither pointless nor irrational. A footballer may be said to act on the principle: 'Let everyone do all he can to make his team score more points than the opposing team.' It is of course impossible for both teams to succeed in doing this, but this does not mean that the principle is in any way incoherent, pointless or irrational. The result of its general adoption is to generate a conflict; but this is in no way irrational if you happen to enjoy that kind of conflict, as footballers undoubtedly do. In any case to object to conflict as such would be to change one's ground. Talk of self-contradiction or incoherence or even perhaps pointlessness looks like an appeal to some formal or logical point. But to say that one ought not to seek conflict is not to make a point about the formal or logical structure of principles, but to lay down a particular moral principle.

There is, however, another possible objection to P 1: that it is a mistranslation, in the way that 'Pull the black lever' may be a mistranslation. For we began with the attitude of the patriot, anxious to promote the interests of his country at whatever cost; and we now have the very different attitude of the games-player: 'Let everyone do his utmost for his side and may the best side win.' The patriot does not want the best side to win, because it is the best; he wants his side to win, because it is his.

Let us, then, try a different formulation of our original P: (P 2) 'Let everyone do what he can to make Australia triumph over all other countries.' This can be applied without change of reference. It is quite possible for Smith the Australian and Jones the Englishman both to aim at making Australia triumph over all other countries, and the success of one does not preclude the success of the other.

It may, however, be objected that this formulation will not do, since it contains a proper name. Proper names do not change their reference; but there is an objection to them, none the less, rather like the objection to 'Pull this lever'. There must be some reason for singling out this lever rather than any other: so the rule is not properly stated unless we have some indication of what that reason is. Similarly there must be some reason for singling out Australia, rather than any other country, as the one whose interests are to be predominant. And if the reason is, for example, that Australia is the most democratic country in the world, or the country with the longest single-span harbour bridge in the world, then it is clear that the proper name can be eliminated in stating the principle.

It is sometimes argued that as a matter of fact proper names always can be eliminated. One can, with a little ingenuity, always find a descriptive phrase which would refer uniquely to the individual one is concerned with. The objection to this, however, is that such formulations would, very often, be mistranslations, in the way that 'pull the black lever' is a mistranslation. The blackness of the lever is not really the reason for pulling it. Similarly the reason the patriot wishes to make his country's interests supreme is not that it is the country with such-and-such intrinsic characteristics, but that it is the country with a certain relational characteristic: the country he was born and bred in. Similarly, the egoist does not really wish to serve the interests of the person who was born in such-and-such a place at such-and-such a time: he wants to serve *his* interests.

Once this is seen, however, it becomes evident that the proper name, too, is a mistranslation. For the patriot does not want to serve Australia's interests because Australia is Australia. Indeed, if 'Australia' is taken simply as a proper name, and not as equivalent to 'the country with characteristics *p, q, r*', it is hard to see what 'because Australia is Australia' could mean. Similarly it is not that the egoist wishes his own interests to predominate because he is Smith: it is rather that he wants Smith's interests to predominate only because Smith is *he*. If it were possible for him to be turned into Jones, then he would, if he were a consistent egoist, want Jones's interests to predominate.

It follows, then, that the first person pronoun cannot be eliminated from either the egoist's or the patriot's principle without misrepresenting those principles. P is, after all, correctly stated as (P 3) 'Let everyone do what he can to make *my* country triumph over all others'. And the corresponding egoistic principle (which we may call E 3) is 'Let everyone do what he can to make *my* interests predominate over everyone else's'.

When it is said that such a principle is not universalizable, what is meant? It is true that the first person pronoun has not been eliminated, but it does not follow that the principle is inapplicable, in the way that the failure to eliminate 'this' or 'now' makes a rule inapplicable. The principle clearly has that kind of universalizability that is analogous to the descriptive universalizability of terms. It is also consequentially universaliz-able: 'my' refers to a relational characteristic that gives the reason behind the principle, and the principle consequently applies to whatever has that relational characteristic. The principle is also socially universalizable: at least in the sense that it is perfectly possible (however unlikely) that others should act on this principle as well as oneself. The patriot intends, not only to do whatever he can to further his own country's interests, but to induce others to further his (not their) country's interests too. Similarly with the egoist.

Earlier, however, we said that principles are universalizable because they imply reasons, and because, if R is a reason for X, it is also a reason for anyone like X in the relevant respects. The patriot's reason for following P 2 will be a reason only for those who resemble him in having been born and bred in Australia. Citizens of other countries, however, have precisely the same reason for trying to promote the interests of their (different) countries. P 1, then, rather than P 2, would seem to be the principle of general application, and the one that most accurately indicates the underlying reason. That is why it is often claimed that P 1 is a universalizable principle, whereas P 2 and *a fortiori* P 3 are not.

Nevertheless, it is important to realize that P 3 and the corresponding egoist principle (E 3), 'Let everyone do whatever he can to further *my* interests', are universalizable, both in the sense that they could be applied by everyone, and in the sense that they indicate a reason for the adoption of the principle by anyone like me in the relevant respect. The relevant respect, it is true, is just *being* I, and this may seem to be a *reductio ad absurdum*, and perhaps a negation, of the whole 'like X in the relevant respects' formula. I do not think, however, that the point can be dismissed so easily.

To anticipate the next chapter: there is danger, throughout the whole contemporary discussion of universalizability, of confusing what is intelligible with what is morally permissible. Universalizability is held to be a logical requirement, and to flout it is regarded as irrational, just because, in some senses of 'universalizable', we would not understand a term or a principle if it were not universalizable. We cannot apply a term or a principle unless we can discriminate between those situations

to which it applies and those to which it does not. If the characteristic *D* is our ground of discrimination, then we are committed to treating alike all things that have *D*. There may in
fact be only one thing that has *D*; but that does not affect the
point. Even if it is *logically* impossible for there to be more than
one thing, *X*, that has *D*, it is nevertheless by virtue of *X*'s
membership of the one-member class, 'things that have *D*',
that the principle applies to *X*.

Now the patriot whose principle is P 3, or the egoist who
applies the corresponding principle, is discriminating between
countries, or between interests, by virtue of a particular relational characteristic: the one referred to by the pronoun 'my'.
This involves discriminating between himself and other men
simply by virtue of the fact that he is he and they are they. No
doubt there are objections to his doing so. But are these objections logical, or moral? The point of saying that P 3 and E 3
are universalizable, in the purely formal sense that they will
apply to anyone else who is *like me* in the 'relevant respect' of
being I, is simply that this ground of discrimination is perfectly
intelligible. It is perfectly proper to protest that the notion of
'similarity in the relevant respects' is being stretched to include
the limiting case in which similarity becomes identity. Say, if
you like, that P 3 and E 3 are not universalizable; but do not
suppose this to mean that they do not denominate a perfectly
intelligible ground of discrimination. The egoist and the patriot
are not being inconsistent or incoherent in the way in which
it would be inconsistent or incoherent to say 'I prefer *X* to *Y*
only because it has *D*, but I do not prefer *X* 1, which also has
D, to *Y*'.

Summarizing what has been said about the universalizability
of rules and principles: rules must be capable of general application, and so it must be possible to state them without the use of
such egocentric particulars ('this', 'here', 'now') as would tie
them to a particular occasion: this may be regarded as the
counterpart of the descriptive universalizability of terms. Rules
which are not merely rules of thumb will indicate or imply

the reason for following them. Such a reason will be a reason for the agent to apply the rule in all relevantly similar situations: this is the counterpart to the consequential universalizability of terms. It will also be a reason for other people like the agent in the relevant respects to apply the rule: this is the counterpart to the social universalizability that consequential terms have.

It has been maintained that the patriot's principle and the egoist's principle have all three types of universalizability, in all the suggested formulations (P 1, P 2, P 3; E 1, E 2, E 3). When it is said that they are not universalizable what is meant is either that there is an implied reference to a relational characteristic and so a change of reference when the principle is applied by different people; or that their application by more than one person will generate conflict; or that the reason one person has for following the principle cannot be a reason for others, except in the purely formal sense that it will be a reason for all who are like him in respect of *being* he.

CHAPTER 16

IMPARTIALITY AND
CONSISTENCY

This somewhat tortuous, and possibly tedious, discussion of the several varieties of universalizability has been made necessary because in current discussion the term is used in a variety of senses, which are seldom clearly distinguished.

Consider the following statements, all from Hare's *Freedom and Reason*:

1. If a person says that a thing is red, he is committed to the view that anything which was like it in the relevant respects would also be red...Moral judgements are, *in the same sense*, universalizable.   (Hare's italics; §2.2)

This is clearly descriptive universalizability. As has already been mentioned, Hare goes on to refer to his own view as 'universal prescriptivism—a combination...of universalism (the view that moral judgements are universalizable) and prescriptivism (the view that they are, at any rate typically, prescriptive)'; and adds that 'descriptive judgements are universalizable in just the same way as, according to my view, moral judgements are' (§ 2.5).

2. Let us suppose...that there are two pictures very like each other. To call one good and the other not commits the speaker to saying that there must be some difference between them which makes them differ in respect of goodness. And if it be granted that there must be some difference between two pictures, one of which is good and the other not, then it follows that if a man calls a picture good, he is committed to calling any other picture good which is exactly similar. Anybody who thinks that all the features of a picture are relevant to its aesthetic appraisal can stop here. But if somebody else thinks that it is possible for some features not to be relevant, he must say that the man is committed also to calling good such pictures as are, while not exactly like the first one, like it in the relevant respects—i.e., those which were his grounds for calling the first one good...

Those who wish to maintain that aesthetic judgements are not universalizable often say that a work of art is 'a unique individual'...Their statement certainly looks as if it were an implicit contradiction of the view that

185

aesthetic judgements are universalizable. But this appearance may be deceptive. Siamese cats are unique individuals—one is never precisely like another; but this does not mean that judgments made at a cat show about their merits are not universalizable. Even if there were only one Siamese cat in the show, a judge who called it a good one would have to admit that *if* there had been another cat in the show like the first one in all, or in the relevant, respects, the second cat would have been a good one too.   (§8.2)

Here it is clearly consequential universalizability that is meant. The second paragraph quoted makes it clear that judgements about the sole member of a class may still be universalizable, in Hare's view.

3. (*a*) It is in their universalizability that value-judgments differ from desires...In this respect wanting is like assenting to a singular imperative, not to a moral or other value-judgement...If I want to do *A* in these circumstances, I am not committed to wanting anyone else placed in exactly or relevantly similar circumstances to do likewise.   (§5.4)

(*b*) ...interests likewise are not universalizable; what it is in one person's interests to have, it is not necessarily in his interest that anyone else should have.   (§9.1)

It is obvious that both desires and interests are universalizable in the sense in which aesthetic judgements are. If I want *X*, and *Y* is exactly like *X* in the relevant respects, it follows that I want *Y*; if I judge *X* to be in my interest, and *Y* is like *X* in the relevant respects, I am committed to saying that *Y* is in my interest too. Hare (though he gives no indication of realizing this) has switched to another sense of universalizability: social universalizability as applied to a consequential term.

4. ...if we enter imaginatively into a hypothetical situation, and think about it *as if* it were going really to happen to us, we logically cannot have desires about it which are different from those which we would have if it *were* going to be real. This is because, whenever we desire something, we desire it because of something about it, and, since being hypothetical and being actual are not, in the required sense, 'things about' objects or events (a hypothetical toothache, exactly like this actual one, *would* hurt as much as this actual one *does* hurt), it is impossible for there to be anything about the hypothetical similar situation which makes us desire something different concerning it. A hypothetical similar situation *is* similar.   (§10.5)

Here Hare is, in effect, admitting that desires are, after all, universalizable in the sense that aesthetic judgements are, that is, consequentially.

5. ...that ideals can and should be diverse does not, as I hope the aesthetic parallel will have made clear, mean that judgements which express ideals are not universalizable, *in the sense in which I have been using the term...* (Hare's italics).

The logical differences between 'ought' and 'right' and 'good'...give us the clue to their different employment. 'Good' has a comparative, 'better', 'ought', and its closely related adjectives, 'right' and 'wrong', normally do not. Moreover, 'good' is probably best defined in terms of its own comparative...It follows from these logical properties of the words and from the universalizability of all value-judgements, that, whereas the judgement that I ought in a certain situation to do a certain thing commits me to the view that no similar person in a precisely similar situation ought to fail to do the same thing, this is not the case with a judgement framed in terms of 'good'. For it is perfectly possible for a person to say, consistently, that he is acting well in going for a run before breakfast, but that his neighbour is not acting ill in staying in bed and closely studying the *Financial Times*. For it is not inconsistent to admit that there may be different ways of life, both of which are good...

So then, our moral language as we have it—universalizability and all—is perfectly well adapted to express the tolerant, diversity-loving views of those like Mr Strawson. We can with consistency say that there are many kinds of good men and good lives. All we are forbidden to do is to say that of two *identical* lives or men, one is good and the other not—it is perfectly in order to say that of two *different* lives or men, both are good.   (§8.6)

Here Hare seems to be saying quite definitely that, in his sense of the term, 'universalizability' is what we have been calling consequential universalizability, and not social universalizability. He is saying in effect that 'right' and 'ought' are (in my terminology) socially universalizable, though 'good' is not, but that, in his sense of the term, all are universalizable, and the difference between them is not to be regarded as a difference in respect of universalizability, but arises from the fact that 'we talk of "a good X" but of "the right X"'; and in general we think it quite natural to speak of there being a large number of good X's, but odd (in most contexts) to speak of there being a large number of right X's'.[1]

[1] *Language of Morals*, §10.1.

It is, of course, perfectly in order for Hare to confine the term 'universalizable' to descriptive and consequential universalizability, if he is prepared to do so consistently. But what he says here seems quite inconsistent with what he says about desires and interests. 'Good', he tells us, is universalizable, and consequently ideals are universalizable, in spite of the fact that I may judge it good to do X without either judging it good for others to do X or implying that they would judge it good to do X, because, in judging something good, I am implying that anything else like it in the relevant respects is also good. Interests, he tells us, are not universalizable, in spite of the fact that in judging something to be in my interest I am implying that anything else like it in the relevant respects is also in my interest, because I may judge it to be in my interest to do X without implying either that it is in my interest for others to do X or that it is in their interest to do X.

6. We saw above that ideals and aesthetic judgements are not just like desires; for there is no universalizability-requirement in the case of desires, whereas there is in the case of both aesthetic judgements and ideals...
...the Nazi is desiring that the Jews should be exterminated; and because the desire is a universal one corresponding to an ideal, he desires that *anyone* having the characteristics which make him want to exterminate Jews should likewise be exterminated. And from this it follows that, if he is sincere and clear-headed, he desires that he himself should be exterminated if he were to come to have the characteristics of Jews. (§9.4)

The difference between an ideal and a desire, Hare is saying, is that one persists in the ideal even if it turns out to one's own disadvantage. He identifies this with consequential universalizability, in a way that is plausible at first sight. But if what a man desires is indeed that Jews should be exterminated, then it does follow, logically, that he desires his own extermination, if he should be a Jew. If, having discovered that his own grandfather was Jewish, and that he is, consequently, a Jew himself according to his criteria, he does not desire his own extermination, the explanation is not, as Hare suggests, that he has some kind of queer non-universalized desire, as distinct from an ideal. There are two possible explanations. One is that what he desires is not that Jews as such should be exterminated, but that, for example, people whom he regards as dangerous rivals should be exterminated. He has, in short, misdescribed (and no doubt misunderstood) his desire: a common enough phenomenon. Alternatively it may be that he does indeed desire the extermination of Jews as Jews, and consequently his own extermination, if he should be a Jew, but that he also desires something else, and desires it more strongly: perhaps just avoidance of suffering for himself. That a desire may conflict with, and be over-ridden by, another desire does not, of course, make it non-universalizable. A moral principle may very well conflict with, and be over-ridden by, another moral principle. It is, I think, because ideals over-ride desires that Hare puts them in the same category as moral principles, and contrasts them with desires and interests. He may be right in doing so, but not in confusing over-ridingness with universalizability.

At times Hare almost seems to be saying that, if the Nazi wants *all* Jews to be exterminated, he has an ideal: if only that *some* shall be, a mere desire. But of course this is too simple. Moral rules, he tells us, can be quite specific and still universalized: 'Tell lies only when...' is universalizable as much as 'Never tell lies...'. To want the extermination of only a particular type of Jew could still be an ideal. It is only when the Nazi exempts those Jews who are his friends, or himself, that Hare refuses to allow that he is motivated by an ideal. Here, as elsewhere, in fact what is called lack of universalizability is really discrimination by reference to relational characteristics.

7. ...if a person has a certain legal obligation, we cannot express this by saying that he *ought* to do such and such a thing, for the reason that 'ought-' judgements have to be universalizable, which, in the strict sense, legal judgements are not. The reason why they are not is that a statement of law always contains an implicit reference to a particular jurisdiction. 'It is illegal to marry one's own sister' means, implicitly, 'It is illegal in (e.g.) England to marry one's own sister'. But 'England' here is a singular term, which prevents the whole proposition being universal; nor is it universalizable, in the sense of committing the speaker to the view that such a marriage would be illegal in any country that was otherwise like England. It is therefore

impossible to use 'ought' in such a statement. The moral judgement that one *ought* not to marry one's sister is, however, universal; it implies no reference to a particular legal system. (§3.3)

It is illuminating that Hare says that it is because 'England' is a singular term that 'illegal' (in England) is not universalizable. This suggests that he is thinking of descriptive or consequential universalizability, both of which are lacking to proper names. But it would be odd to say that 'illegal' is not a descriptive term. And indeed it is false that 'it is illegal in England' does not commit one to the view that 'such a marriage would be illegal in any country that was otherwise like England'. It would be illegal in any country like England *in the relevant respects*: viz. any country with a legal prohibition against marrying one's sister.

This, it may be objected, is not to be *otherwise* like England. But for 'illegal' to have descriptive universalizability, to be universalizable in the sense that 'red' is, it is only necessary that 'it is illegal to marry one's sister' should imply that anything like marrying one's sister in the relevant respect (in this case, in being forbidden by the laws of a particular country) is illegal in that country.

It cannot even be said that 'illegal' lacks consequential universalizability. For, when a judge or a lawyer tries to decide whether a given act (such as marrying one's sister) is illegal, he applies certain criteria: resemblance to the acts that figure in leading cases, conformity to the descriptions in the relevant statutes, and so on. In coming to a decision, he certainly implies that any action to which these criteria apply will have the further characteristic of being illegal, that is, of being liable to punishment by the courts, and so on. This would seem to be little different from deciding by certain criteria (motive, consequences, etc.) that an action is right, and so deserving of praise, emulation and so on.

When Hare says that 'illegal' is not universalizable he is confusing these types of universalizability with the social universalizability that is appropriate to rules. But 'Refrain from the illegal act of marrying your sister' is socially universalizable in that it would apply to anyone like the speaker in the relevant respect: viz. being subject to the laws of England. One suspects that Hare's real point here is that this involves discriminating between people by reference to a relational and in a sense an adventitious characteristic. Naturally enough reference to proper names often indicates relational characteristics, and this is one reason why lack of universalizability is often confused with universalizability in which the 'relevant respect' is a relational characteristic.

Two incidental comments may be made on this passage. First, it is surely doubtful that 'ought' cannot be used in a legal context. 'According to the law, one ought not to marry one's sister' is a perfectly normal and intelligible English sentence. Secondly, while the 'ought' here is of course not a moral 'ought', this is not because of its lack of universal application. For suppose that in fact all countries did have a law against marrying one's sister (as, for all I know, they may have). Or suppose that there were a single world government (an extension of the United Nations perhaps) imposing laws on all mankind. 'It is illegal to marry one's sister' would not then have an implied reference to the legal system of just one country. But the appropriateness of using 'ought' would not be affected. Hare may or may not be right in saying that 'ought' cannot be used of legal (as distinct from moral) rights and duties. But, if he is right, it would not seem to be because legal rights and duties are restricted in their application.

What, it may be asked, do these shifts of meaning matter, since the precise sense of 'universalizable' is usually clear from the context? The answer is that it makes a great deal of difference whether universalizability is a logical requirement or a moral one. Contemporary moral philosophers are reluctant to embrace non-naturalism because of its metaphysical implications; but naturalism is equally unacceptable because it seems to lead straight to subjectivism and perhaps to ethical nihilism. In this situation, as was pointed out in an earlier chapter, some of them have turned to the universalizability thesis as providing a middle way between objectivism and subjectivism.

It is essential, if this argument is to hold, that universalizability should be a purely formal, logical feature of moral utterances, and not itself a moral principle. As we have seen, a moral principle may enable us to differentiate between the moral and the immoral, but not between the moral and the non-moral; for behaviour which fails to conform to a moral principle can hardly be outside the sphere of morality altogether; if it were, moral principles would not be applicable to it at all. To claim, then, that a statement or a rule of conduct that cannot be universalized is, by definition, not a moral statement or a moral rule, is to claim that the principle of universalizability is not itself a moral principle.

Moreover, if it were a moral principle, all the traditional questions would arise about it. Is it, we could ask, merely that we have a deep-seated preference for accepting as moral principles only universalizable ones, or is it a non-empirical, objective truth, known by intuition, that moral principles must be universalizable? It is in order to avoid this dilemma that it is claimed that it is logically true that moral principles are universalizable, and that it is in some sense irrational to put forward a non-universalizable principle as a moral one. My contention is that this thesis is plausible only so long as many quite different things are all being referred to as 'universalizability'. Certainly it is irrational to say both that X is red and that Y is the same colour as X (like X in the relevant respect) but not red. It is by no means so certain that it is irrational to want to make exceptions in one's own favour.

It may indeed be said that a breach of any of the types of universalizability we have distinguished, whether of terms or of rules, would be irrational. The descriptive, the consequential and the social universalizability of terms are all necessary consequences of the use of language to communicate, and it is hard to see how we could use words at all unless it is understood: (*a*) that if a term applies to X because of some characteristic of X, then it must apply to anything else with the same character-istic; (b) that if possession of a certain set of characteristics justifies the use of a further term in addition to those terms which refer directly to those characteristics, then this term must apply to anything with those characteristics; (c) that those with whom we communicate must use and understand terms in the same way as we do. The first and second of these are indeed analytically true.

Since the universalizability of rules was found to be the counterpart of the universalizability of terms, the same may be said of it. Certainly there would seem to be some kind of con-tradiction involved in the notion of a rule that cannot be applied to more than one situation: it would not then be a rule. The counterpart to descriptive universalizability is simply that rules must be capable of application. The counterpart of con-sequential universalizability, however, was said to be the re-quirement that a rule should not be a rule of thumb, and it may be argued that rules of thumb are not irrational. Certainly it is not irrational to follow a rule of thumb (such as 'Always pull the black lever') provided that such a rule could be translated (perhaps by someone else with greater knowledge) into a rule that was not a rule of thumb. To follow a rule of thumb in-capable of such translation, however, is to indulge in meaning-less ritual. Certainly this is not irrational in the sense of in-volving a contradiction: it is, however, irrational behaviour in the sense of being random or arbitrary. The counterpart of social universalizability need not delay us: if a rule is to be applied by X, and there is no relevant difference between X and Y, it is clearly irrational (in the sense of inconsistent) to suggest that the rule should not be applied by Y.

So far, then, it would seem that the distinctions we have been making between different types of universalizability do nothing to upset the contention that universalizability is a requirement of rationality. It has, however, appeared from our discussion that the instances of lack of universalizability generally cited are really something different: viz. instances of discrimination between two things or situations by reference to a certain kind of relational characteristic rather than to intrinsic ones.

Consider, for example, what Hughes says about the difference between expressing annoyance and making a moral judgement. He puts this, it will be remembered, in the form of a distinction between 'condemns' and 'morally condemns'.

I am maintaining, then, that whereas the sentence (i) 'whoever condemns *X* also condemns whatever he regards as similar to *X* in the relevant respects' expresses a contingent (and incidentally false) proposition, the sentence (ii) 'whoever *morally* condemns *X* also morally condemns whatever he regards as similar to *X* in the relevant respects' expresses a logically necessary truth and one that is elucidatory, or at least partially elucidatory, of the meaning of the word 'morally'.[1]

Now, if you say 'I am annoyed with *X* because of its characteristics *p*, *q*, *r*' you do of course imply that the same characteristics in *Y*, or in *X* on another occasion, will also annoy you. Nevertheless, Hughes is right when he says that we do not think that you have contradicted yourself if half an hour later you say that *X* no longer annoys you although its characteristics have not changed in the meantime. The explanation is, of course, that strictly speaking the cause of your annoyance is not just *X*'s characteristics *p*, *q*, *r*, but those characteristics in conjunction with your preexisting attitude. The point is a familiar one about causation. We often distinguish between 'the cause' and 'the standing conditions', but the distinction, though useful, is largely arbitrary. The most satisfactory account of causation is one that takes the cause to be the whole set of conditions that are necessary and sufficient for the occurrence of the effect, including both the 'standing conditions' and those more changeable features which we are likely to call '*the* cause'. To say, then, that you are annoyed by *X* because of its characteristics *p*, *q*, *r* is certainly to make a universalizable statement; but the 'relevant respects' here include your own mood as well as *p*, *q*, *r*.

[1] G. E. Hughes, 'Moral Condemnation', in A. I. Melden (ed.), *Essays in Moral Philosophy* (University of Washington Press, 1958), pp. 108–34.

Now let us suppose that *X* is a child, who interrupts you when you are working. Normally you tolerate such interruptions, but, on this occasion, being in a bad mood, you smack the child. We would probably think this unfair. Certainly if you have two children, both of whom interrupt you, and you smack one (because you happen to be feeling in a bad mood at the moment when he bursts in) but not the other, we would think this unjust. On the other hand, if you smack both children impartially, in order to teach them not to disturb adults when they are busy, we would not think that you were behaving unjustly, whether or not we approved of your action on the whole. Moreover, we might well say, in Hughes's terminology, that in the first case you condemned the child who interrupted you, but did not morally condemn him; in the second case your condemnation was moral condemnation.

But this suggests that Hughes has misdescribed the difference between the two. It is not that moral condemnation is universalizable while condemnation is not: it is rather that, with condemnation, we regard a change of mood as 'a relevant respect', and so one which can make two situations relevantly dissimilar: with moral condemnation we do not regard a change of mood as a relevant respect.

A similar point can be made about Gellner's example of romantic love. When Edwin falls in love with Angelina because of her characteristics *p, q, r*, and then fails to fall in love with the next girl he meets who has characteristics *p, q, r*, there is a difference in the relevant circumstances: namely, that Edwin's affections are already engaged. It is (to put it mildly) socially permissible in our culture for him to discriminate between the two girls by reference to this relational characteristic ('being encountered by me when I was not already in love'). That kissing goes by favour and that moral condemnation (including the punishment of children) does not, is, of course, a highly important social requirement: to understand it will certainly help us to understand a good deal about morality. My point is simply that the rule which embodies this requirement is itself a moral rule. It is gravely misleading to treat it as a formal, logical characteristic of moral statements.

It has already been suggested that egoism and patriotism depend on principles that are, after all, universalizable, but whose universalization requires discrimination by virtue of relational characteristics. I shall recapitulate the points already made. We distinguished the following principles, as variants of patriotism:

P 1. Let everyone do what will make his country triumph over all others.

P 2. Let everyone do what will make X triumph over all other countries (where X is the name of a country).

P 3. Let everyone do what will make my country triumph over all other countries.

Similarly, the egoist's principle may be stated in three ways:

E 1. Let everyone do what will make his own interests prevail over everyone else's.

E 2. Let everyone do what will make X's interests prevail over everyone else's (where X is the egoist's name).

E 3. Let everyone do what will make my interests prevail over everyone else's.

Each of these contains either an uneliminated personal pronoun or an uneliminated proper name. This does not, however, seem to justify their being called non-universalizable: indeed, the 'let everyone . . .' would seem to be enough to make them universal prescriptions, as Hare requires. It may indeed be argued that P 1 and E 1 are not universalizable, on the ground that, since the interests in question change with every person who applies the principle, it is not really the same principle that is being applied. P 1, when applied by an Australian, yields one P 2 principle, and, when applied by an Englishman, yields a different P 2 principle. Yet it is usually claimed that it is P 1 and E 1 that are universalizable, whereas the others are not. Hare, for example, says quite unequivocally, 'If a patriot thinks that he owes certain duties to his own country, but agrees that other people owe similar duties to their countries, his maxim is of type U ("one owes such-and-such duties to one's country") . . . But if he thinks that other people do not owe the same duties to their countries, then—unless he points to relevant differences between his country and others—his maxim is not of type U.'[1]

We may well suspect that it is a moral, and not a logical, consideration that is being invoked here. Certainly it is unfair to expect both you and me to make my country's interests the prime consideration, and much fairer to allow each of us to consider his own country's interests. But fairness is, of course, a moral consideration. Hare, indeed, seems to distinguish between P 1 and E 1 here: in the passage quoted he is talking only about patriotism, and everything he says about egoism would suggest that he does not regard E 1 as 'a type U maxim'. This may well be significant, since, while E 1 and P 1 do not differ formally, many people would say that, from a moral point of view, considering one's own interests is importantly different from considering the interests of one's country.

Nevertheless, there is a case for saying that P 1 and E 1 are more rational than P 2 or P 3, or E 2 or E 3. Before stating it, however, I shall consider a wider, and obviously relevant, question: Is it irrational to discriminate between two things either by virtue of a relational, as distinct from an intrinsic, characteristic, or on the grounds that a particular proper name applies to one but not to the other? If it is, then all six of the principles under discussion are irrational.

William Godwin, it will be remembered, argued that the rule about keeping promises is irrational. We ought, he says, to do an action or to refrain from doing it because of the nature of the action, not because it has the adventitious characteristic of having-been-promised-by-me. The point can be put in the form of a dilemma: either the action is right, in which case I ought to do it whether I have promised to or not; or it is not, in which case I ought not to do it whether I have promised to or not. In either case the promise is irrelevant.

On much the same grounds Godwin argued that you ought to save Archbishop Fénelon from the burning building instead

---

[1] Aristotelian Society, *Proceedings*, LV (1954–5), 299.

of his chambermaid (on the supposition that Fénelon had more to contribute to the general happiness) even if the chambermaid should be your mother. 'What magic is there', he asked, 'in the pronoun "my", that should justify us in overturning the decisions of impartial truth?'

These arguments are certainly not simply silly. We may well be made uneasy by the reflection: 'If it had been Jane instead of Mary I happened to meet at that party...' or 'if I had happened to be born in Russia instead of Britain...'. But one's uneasiness is due to a reluctance to admit that one is the sport of circumstances, that one's aspirations and desires are, as Kant put it, 'heteronomous', at least partly due to factors outside one's control. If we *are* the sport of circumstances, however, there is nothing irrational about acknowledging that fact and taking account of it. Our desires are no less our desires, and no less important to us, because they have this kind of origin.

This consideration applies to Godwin's remarks about one's mother rather than to his remarks about one's promises. Here the point is a different one. It is irrational to promise to do a particular action rather than another unless the promised action has some desirable feature that the alternative has not: in which case it is that feature, and not the fact that it has been promised, that constitutes the reason for doing it. The general point (whether or not it applies to promises, where the issue is complicated by the need, in society, to know how others are going to act) is the one that arises about proper names. It is irrational to single out Smith instead of Jones unless Smith has some characteristic that Jones has not: in which case the ground of discrimination can be stated without bringing in the proper name at all.

Does it follow, however, that the characteristic in question must not be a relational one? If there are any doubts about 'promised-by-me' as a ground of discrimination, they do not arise because concern for promises would make us the sport of circumstances, but rather for the opposite reason: since promises are within my control, I must have some reason for promising this rather than that. But there is not the same sort of case for saying that 'because she is my mother' is a less rational ground of discrimination than 'because he will contribute more to the general happiness'. Each of these is, indeed, a relational characteristic. On the other hand, 'I will save the chambermaid because she is a woman', or 'because she has red hair', would certainly be regarded by Godwin as irrational, though here intrinsic characteristics are made the basis of discrimination.

We encounter here a familiar problem. 'Everyone except Jones must pay taxes' or 'Everyone except the red-haired must pay taxes' may both be deemed irrational, and for the same reason. Why single out Jones? Why single out the red-haired? But 'everyone except those with incomes of less than £500 a year must pay taxes' is not thought irrational, because here we can answer the 'why single out...?' question. But suppose our questioner keeps on pressing us. Why single out those to whom greater hardship will be caused? At some point, of course, we have to stop offering reasons, and say something like 'Minimizing hardship is an ultimate principle with me'. But now the obvious question is 'Why not say that it is an ultimate principle that people with red hair should not pay taxes? Or that Jones should not?'

However these questions are answered (and I do not deny that they can be answered), it is by no means obvious that some such answer as 'because I am Jones' or 'because Jones is my best friend' could not serve as the ultimate principle we are looking for. For suppose I say 'I do all that I can to save myself pain'. No doubt I shall want to qualify this: there may be occasions when I think pain to myself the lesser of two evils. This principle, then, need not be ultimate in the sense of over-riding every other principle. But it is ultimate in the sense that I shall always regard pain-to-me as an evil, not because of its consequences but because of what it is in itself. And the reason for this is not that I am fair-haired, or a British citizen, or a member of any other class of men. I could not, without distorting my actual motive, replace 'pain to myself' by 'pain to all

X's', whatever value we give to X. The reason I want to avoid pain to myself is just that I am I.

Perhaps I would also be prepared to say 'I do all I can to prevent pain to all men' or perhaps 'to all sentient creatures'. But this does not mean that the first principle is merely a special case of the second. (Failure to recognize this is responsible for a notorious crux in the utilitarianism of Bentham and Mill.) For my own pain is, for me, in a special category. This is just a brute fact, and quite a central one.

Anyone who disputes this may be invited to consider the following situation: Jones and Brown are both questioned by the police. Jones lies, to save himself. Brown lies, to save Jones. Does each man act from the same motive? In a sense, they do: for the motive is to save Jones. But most of us would say, nevertheless, that the impulse to save one's own skin is a very different motive from the impulse to save a friend. One's concern for oneself is not just an instance of one's concern for mankind in general.

So far, then, our contention has been that it is not necessarily irrational to make relational characteristics, and particularly a relation to oneself, a ground of discrimination. In particular, what has just been said provides a sufficient answer to the argument that it is nonsensical to stretch the 'anyone like X in the relevant respect' formula to cover the case of being like X in *being* X. To discriminate between two persons, X and Y, just because X is X and Y is Y is not like discriminating arbitrarily between two peas in a pod or two screws turned out by the same factory. Respect for the individual as such is often expressed by saying that every individual is unique; but this actually suggests the opposite of what is meant, since it implies that it is not individuality as such, but some further ground of difference, that deserves respect. Even if we can find no difference at all between two identical twins, say, it does not follow that we are entitled to treat them as if they were interchangeable, as if, for example, to give one of them two treats were the same as treating each of them once.

What this brings out is that 'Treat two things alike unless there is some relevant difference between them' is fundamentally ambiguous: the appeal may be to fairness or it may be to interchangeability. If two things are interchangeable it is irrational to go to great pains to choose one rather than the other. If you hold up the queue at the lunch counter while you hunt for your favourite knife and fork in the cutlery tray when all the knives, and all the forks, are exactly alike, you are, to put it mildly, being neurotic. Here it does not matter which you choose, just because there is no difference between them: any will do. But, when it is said that you ought not to discriminate between your children (say) the point is quite a different one. It is not that it does not matter which you choose, so any will do. On the contrary, it is just because it matters a lot (to them) which you choose (to give the present to, let us say) that you should try to treat them alike. It is not that the fact that they are separate individuals is a matter of no importance, and so one which no rational man would take account of. It is just because one does take account of it that the question of fairness arises.

It follows that it is not irrational to treat an individual as a one-member class, constituted by the mere fact that he is a separate individual. In particular, the fact that I am I and you are you is not (like the fact that this knife is this one, but that knife is that one) an irrational ground of discrimination. It would indeed be irrational not to recognize the mere distinctness of persons as an important difference, as the example of the two perjurors, Smith and Jones, brings out.

This same example does, however, provide us with an argument for saying that P 1 or E 1 is more rational than P 2 or P 3, or E 2 or E 3. 'To save Jones' provides Jones with one motive, and Smith with quite a different motive. If Smith's reason for lying were the same as Jones's, he would lie, not to save Jones, but to save Smith. Similarly, that this country is my country or this interest my interest does not provide you with the same reason for acting as it does me. If you act for the same reason, you will promote your interests, or your country's interests, not mine.

Does it follow that principles of the P 3 and E 3 type are irrational? (We may ignore P 2 and E 2, which were earlier shown to be mistranslations of P 3 and E 3.) Is it, in other words, irrational to act from one motive yourself, and to re-quire other people to act from a different motive? Certainly, if you regard your own motive as a rational one, then you must admit that it is rational for others to act from the corresponding motive. If it is rational for you to put your country's interests first, then it is rational for me to put first the interests, not of your country, but of mine. It is on this ground that P 1 is said to be rational and P 3 not. The same argument will, of course, apply to E 1 and E 3.

But does it follow from this that it is irrational to *want* other people, as well as yourself, to further the interests of your country? All that follows is that, if you do want this, you are wanting other people to be irrational. But there seems no reason to say that this is itself irrational. No doubt it is irrational (it is certainly arrogant) to expect to be the only rational person in one's community; but it is not irrational to try to induce other people to act irrationally, if one can.

But, it will be said, suppose someone does do this. If he genuinely thinks that his own motive is a rational one, he will respect other people only so far as they fail to fall in with his wishes. The patriotic Englishman, for example, may well try to induce a German to serve England's interests rather than Germany's; but, if he succeeds, he will despise the German. He will, of course, praise those Germans who fall in with his wishes and dispraise those who do not; but, in his secret thoughts, he will despise the pliant Germans and approve of the recalcitrant ones. Now the principles according to which a man approves of actions (even if he lies about what he approves) are his moral principles. Our patriot, then, approves only of those who act from the same motive as himself, and disapproves (though he *says* he approves) of those who act from different motives. His moral principle, then, so far as he is rational, is P 1 and not P 3.

This is, however, not quite accurate. For our patriot may have nothing but contempt for the P 1 patriot, so far as he is committed to saying 'Let the best man win!' 'Away with this namby-pamby stuff!' he may say. 'The man I respect is the man who does his damnedest to make *his* side win, and induces others, so far as he can, to help him.' So that, even as a moral principle (that is, as determining what one approves of) P 3 is different from P 1.

We must, I think, distinguish between three possibilities:

1. I may want X, approve of my wanting X, approve of others wanting X, and also want others to want X.
2. I may want X, approve of my wanting X, and approve of others wanting X, but not want others to want X.
3. I may want X, and approve of my wanting X, but disapprove of others wanting X.

The problems we have been considering arise when my obtaining X is incompatible with others also obtaining X. Egoism and patriotism are concerned with just this kind of situation. Applying these three types of principle, we get the different kinds of egoist and patriot already mentioned. The first says, in effect, 'Everyone ought to put his own interests (the interests of his country) first, and ignore those of others'. The second says, in effect, 'Since it is reasonable for me to put my interests (the interests of my country) first, it is reasonable for others to put their interests (the interests of their country) first; but since their aim, though quite as reasonable as mine, is incompatible with mine, I shall do my best to stop them from pursuing it.'

There is nothing irrational about either of these policies. They may or may not be desirable. But they cannot be ruled out as muddle-headed, in the way the third man is muddle-headed. For he does not recognize that what is reasonable for him must be reasonable for anyone else in the same circumstances. He will not, like the patriotic Englishman described above, only *say* that he approves of the German whom he has induced to serve Britain's interests instead of Germany's: he really will feel towards the German's action exactly as he feels towards his own. He is not, like the other type of patriot, cynical and Machiavellian: morally, he is no doubt less reprehensible. But he is certainly less rational. And he, alone of the three, really is ignoring the universalizability principle.

Indeed, he is probably too muddle-headed to exist. There are, of course, plenty of muddle-headed patriots; but it is doubtful if any of them admit to themselves that their reason for serving, say, Britain's interests is just that it happens to be their country. They are much more likely to persuade themselves that their devotion is due to some intrinsic (as distinct from relational) characteristic of Britain: perhaps that it is a democratic country. If this is self-deception, it is still highly significant that self-deception should be necessary here. For once we acknowledge to ourselves that something is a reason for us, we can hardly fail to acknowledge that it will also be a reason for anyone else in our circumstances.

This irrational egoist or patriot does not, it should be noted, correspond to any of the types (followers of E 1, E 2 or E 3, or of P 1, P 2 or P 3) mentioned earlier. None of these is irrational: and E 3 and P 3 are no more irrational than E 1 and P 1. It is not irrational, that is to say, to discriminate between two things by reference to a relational characteristic, and, in particular, by means of a relation to oneself. The objection to this is a moral objection, not a logical one.

Broadly, we may distinguish between two quite different requirements which have become inextricably confused in the universalizability thesis: a logical requirement, which we may call the principle of consistency, and a moral requirement, which we may call the principle of impartiality. The different kinds of universalizability, descriptive, consequential and social (which have themselves been confused with one another), are all consequences of the demand for consistency: consistency in the use of language as a means of communication. To dis-

criminate between two things by means of a relational characteristic, and in particular an agent-relational characteristic—a
relation to oneself—is not to be inconsistent, since it is quite
possible to apply this basis of discrimination consistently, but it
is of course to be partial, biased in one's own favour.

It follows that the universalizability thesis will not enable us
to find a middle way between subjectivism and objectivism.
The contention is that, since universalizability is part of the
meaning of 'moral', it is not possible (*logically* impossible) to
have moral beliefs or attitudes that are not applied impartially
to all men. This accounts for all that is sound in objectivism,
and enables us to embrace an aseptic subjectivism. It also makes
it possible to meet the objection that, according to subjectivism,
moral argument should be impossible. Hare maintains that,
'once the logical character of moral concepts is understood,
there can be useful and compelling moral argument even
between people who have, before it begins, no substantive
moral principles in common'.[1] This is because one disputant
can point out to the other the consequences of universalizing
the moral principles he does hold, in the hope of finding one
that may be unacceptable to him.

Against this position, I have argued in these pages:

1. The characteristic by means of which we distinguish the
moral from the non-moral cannot itself be a moral characteristic, but must be morally neutral. The three types of universalizability are indeed morally neutral, but, since they are
common to almost all terms (and their counterparts to all
principles), they will not serve to distinguish the moral from
the non-moral. The principle of impartiality, which is confused
with universalizability, is not morally neutral, but is itself a
moral principle. Hence it is exposed to all the traditional
questions about the nature and justification of moral principles,
and can hardly be said to make those questions otiose. It is
only because this moral principle has been confused with the
various types of universalizability that its nature has been

---

[1] *Freedom and Reason*, p. 187, § 10.1.

said to be logical, and its justification to rest on the axioms of logic.

2. The principle of impartiality is a very fundamental moral principle, and it may very well be incapsulated in our use of moral terms. To that extent Hare is right in saying that it is part of what we mean by 'moral'. The difficulty is that, although there is very good ground for saying that 'universalizability' (or the principle of impartiality that Hare confuses with it) is a defining characteristic of morality, morality (which is a quite complex phenomenon known through experience) has other defining characteristics as well. In particular, we regard our moral principles as over-riding any others that conflict with them. Now it is undoubtedly true that the principles that most of us accept as over-riding are universalizable. But this is a synthetic truth. The danger of insisting that 'universalizability' is part of the meaning of morality is that we may be led to suppose that it is a necessary truth.

I believe that those who put forward the universalizability thesis have fallen into this trap. When it is said that only universalizable principles are moral, the implication is smuggled in that only universalizable principles can be over-riding ones. Otherwise the purely formal logical principle will not do the job it is wanted for. For example, it is not true that two men without any 'substantive moral principles in common' can have 'useful and compelling' moral argument once they have grasped the logic of moral terms. For such argument will be neither useful nor compelling unless the disputants agree that one ought to guide one's life by (accept as over-riding) only universalizable principles. It is *that* principle, not the purely verbal point about what most people in our culture call 'moral', that gets the argument going: and it is a substantive moral principle.

As such, it needs justification. If universalizability is taken as the sole defining characteristic of morality then the question 'Why guide our lives by moral principles, and not, for example, by selfish ones?' does demand an answer. The reason that the question seems odd, and perhaps senseless, is that the question 'Why guide our lives by over-riding principles?' is an odd one, by virtue of the meaning of the word 'over-riding'. But it is not odd by virtue of the meaning of the word 'moral', except to the extent that moral implies 'over-riding' as well as 'universalizable'. In ordinary usage 'moral' carries both these implications, just as 'courageous' implies both 'commendable' and 'selflessly disregarding one's own danger'. But, just as it makes sense to ask 'Is it, after all, commendable to disregard one's own danger for the sake of the safety of others?', so it makes sense to ask 'Are universalizable principles, after all, the only over-riding ones?' In both cases we may have little doubt about the answer: the point is simply that the question may be asked. It is not made otiose by an examination of the logic of courage, or of morality. As Hare himself remarks, 'the mere existence of a certain conceptual apparatus cannot compel any-body to accept any particular evaluation, although it is more difficult to break away from evaluations which are incapsulated in the very language which we use'.[1]

[1] *Freedom and Reason*, p. 191, §10.3.

MORALITY AS OVER-RIDING

As we have seen, the naturalist is faced with the question 'If morality is to be explained in terms of a particular kind of attitude or feeling, how do these moral attitudes or feelings differ from non-moral ones?' So far I have argued that he cannot answer this by saying that moral attitudes (beliefs, etc.) are universalizable, and have suggested instead that he should say that moral attitudes or beliefs are over-riding. This answer at once raises a number of objections, with which I shall now try to deal.

First objection: 'over-riding' is, like 'universalizable', itself a moral term.

Universalizability, I have argued, presupposes moral concepts, admittedly in a somewhat indirect way. The difficulty is that universalizability, in the relevant sense, is itself a moral requirement, and not merely a logical one. It depends, not on interchangeability and indifference, but on such concepts as fairness and the importance of the individual. Now to say that a desire is an over-riding one for X, it may be argued, is not to say that X always gratifies this desire in preference to any conflicting desires, but only that he believes that he ought to gratify it. Clearly the naturalist needs to say that 'believes that he ought to gratify it' is just a way of saying 'will feel guilt or remorse unless he gratifies it'. But are not 'guilt' and 'remorse' moral terms? Can we give a purely phenomenological account of guilt and remorse as feelings? Are not they, in fact, feelings of regret accompanied by the conviction that we have done those things we ought not to have done, or left undone those things we ought to have done?

It is tempting to answer this by saying, as many psychologists have said, that guilt comes from 'internalizing' the voice of parental authority. The child knows that he will be punished, or admonished, if he does certain kinds of action. Thereafter he feels uneasy when he does them. 'Guilt' is simply the name we give to this distinctive kind of uneasiness.

The objection to this account is that our feelings of guilt are far from being automatic echoes of the parental voice. Or, if they are, then this kind of guilt (an emotional reaction due to conditioning) is not the same as the conviction that one ought to do so-and-so. The difference may be illustrated by the following case: *X* has been brought up in a socialist family, and has for many years been an active worker for the Labour party. In time, however, he comes to change his views, convinced that socialism is incompatible with individual freedom. The time comes when, for the first time, he casts a vote against the party with which he has for so long identified himself. As he leaves the polling-booth, he is overwhelmed by an acute feeling of misery. He feels a criminal and a traitor. His emotion is undoubtedly guilt; and yet he knows that he has pondered long and earnestly before making his decision, and is still convinced that that decision was the right one.

This example makes it clear that guilt, as an emotional reaction, is not only not the same as, but may even conflict with, the intellectual conviction that one has done wrong. Now, we have said that a policy is an over-riding one when we either allow it to prevail over a conflicting one, or, if we do not, feel guilt. It is clear that, for *X* in our example, support for socialism was not an over-riding policy. The guilt that accompanies failure to support an over-riding policy, then, is not the purely emotional reaction, but the feeling that accompanies the considered conviction that one has done something wrong. But in that case, clearly, we have failed to give an account of guilt that does not involve irreducibly moral concepts.

But perhaps the psychologist's account is not wholly wrong, but only over-simplified. Certainly there is more to guilt than a simple conditioned reflex. It is not just that we have come to feel uneasy whenever we find ourselves boasting, or answering someone rudely, or doing any of the other things for which we were once scolded, in the same way as we have learned to jump when we hear a motor horn just behind us. Certainly we can, and do, reason about what is right and wrong. Moreover, we may reach conclusions quite at variance with what our parents and teachers taught us.

It may still be true, none the less, that, as a result not only of parental admonitions but of all the other social pressures to which we are subject, each of us gradually builds up an image of himself as the sort of person who always behaves in such-and-such a way: who is never knowingly unkind perhaps, or insensitive to what others are feeling; or who never makes the flat, obvious, boring remark; or who never leaves things undone out of mere laziness, but is unsparing of himself and others. We come, in short, to form ideals. Ideals vary, as people vary. But they have this in common, that we feel a peculiar uneasiness when we detect ourselves not living up to them. This is true even if we are impatient of ideals, and pride ourselves on not being too earnest and not taking ourselves too seriously; for, in the sense in which I am using the term, that too is an ideal.

But, it will be objected, not all of these are moral ideals. Morality is narrower than this account would suggest. It is also wider; for not all moral judgements are concerned with breaches of ideals. Both these objections raise wider questions, which will be discussed later. At the moment, the task is to give a naturalistic account of guilt: one, that is to say, which does not simply amount to a conviction that one has done what one ought not to do, where 'ought' is an irreducible moral term. The suggestion so far is that it is a psychological and sociological fact that we do form ideals of the kind described, that we have a peculiar feeling of uneasiness when we do not live up to them (a phenomenon itself easily explicable) and that 'guilt' is the term used for such a feeling.

It is true, however, that personal ideals are not the whole of morality. Apart altogether from evaluating his own actions, and asking himself whether they are of the kind likely to be done by the sort of person he would like to be, a man comes to evaluate states of affairs. He develops, perhaps, what Russell calls 'impersonal desires': preferences (for example) for a world in which men live at peace with one another, or in which they may speak their minds without fear of punishment, or in which they treat each other as equals, or in which they have a due respect for their social superiors. These preferences, though distinct from personal ideals, are connected with them, since a man with such a preference is likely to pride himself on being the sort of person who tries hard to bring about the state of affairs he favours. Nevertheless, it is important to distinguish between the two. When a man asks himself whether a given course of conduct is right, he is not always asking a question about the character, or motives, of the agent. He is concerned, at least as often, with the consequences of the action.

Both personal ideals and desires for favoured states of affairs may come into conflict with other desires. It is, of course, an essential part of my thesis that what distinguishes them from other desires is simply that, on reflection, we desire them more. But this is quite compatible with finding it very hard indeed to gratify the stronger desire, and being strongly tempted to yield to the weaker desire. To say that I would much rather be the sort of person who rises early each morning and gets in a solid day's work at his desk than the sort who idly fritters away his time is quite compatible with my finding it very hard indeed to get up and very easy to neglect my work in favour of reading a light novel.

But, it will be objected, does not this merely go to show that your internal conflict is misdescribed when it is represented as being between a weaker and a stronger desire? The stronger desire is just the one that conquers in the end. The conflict here is between two different *kinds* of desire: for comfort and for the right course of conduct. Either may turn out to be the stronger, on a given occasion: it is not that that makes one of them a moral desire.

Natural as this objection is, it is not conclusive. To say that a given course of conduct is the right one may still be merely to say that it is the one I prefer, on reflection and most of the

time. Consider another example. Suppose that I go into a shop
to buy a pair of shoes. I know that my feet are an unorthodox
shape and that, unless I am very careful, I shall get a pair that do
not fit and will cause me considerable discomfort later on. But
at the second or third shop I grow tired of endlessly trying on
shoes and resisting the assurances of the assistants that they will
very soon stretch into the right shape. I know that I really
ought to go out of the shop and continue the search in yet
another one. But, tired of the whole tedious business, I allow
myself, against my better judgement, to be persuaded that one
of the pairs will do. Later, when the shoes begin to pinch, I
regret this decision bitterly and upbraid myself for my spineless-
ness and laziness.

Now what do I mean when I tell myself, as I certainly shall,
that I have done the wrong thing, that I ought not to have
bought those shoes? Only that I have not done what (on
reflection and most of the time) I most want to do. My desire to
save myself the trouble of shopping and my desire to have
shoes that fit are not, in the relevant sense, different kinds of
desire. Each is concerned with my own comfort. The question
between them is simply whether I want to gratify one more
than I want to gratify the other. Yet this example is a precise
parallel to the first one. In each the desire that is (in a perfectly
intelligible sense) the weaker proves to be stronger at the cru-
cial moment. In each I quite naturally use such expressions as 'I
ought not to have done that'; in each I blame myself for lack of
will power.

So far, then, the suggestion is that guilt is the distinctive
feeling that results from not getting something one wants
because one has not tried hard enough to attain it; usually
because one has allowed another, lesser, desire to get in the way.
But, it may be asked, has not the definition now become circular? We began by defining a moral attitude (conviction,
policy) as an over-riding one. To say that it is over-riding is
to say that we either follow it in preference to a conflicting
policy, or, if we do not, feel guilt. And what is guilt? The

emotion we feel when we do not allow an over-riding policy to prevail.

The circularity here is only apparent. It just is the case that men regard some objectives as peculiarly important, and that they decide to suppress desires which conflict with those objectives. It is also the case that they pride themselves on being persons of a particular kind. Such objectives and such self-idealizations are, I have suggested, over-riding, in the sense that they represent what we most want. It is also the case that failure to live up to such ideals, or failure, as the result of lack of effort, to attain these objectives, is attended by a quite distinctive emotion.

But it will at once be asked, does not the phrase 'peculiarly important' beg the question, and indeed give the whole game away? What is 'peculiar' about the importance attached to these objectives or to these images of oneself except that they are felt to be *morally* important?

There is, in short, no way of overcoming the first objection except by saying quite flatly that the over-riding desire is the strongest desire. Certainly it may not prove strongest (that is, prevail) on a given occasion; but it must nevertheless be the desire that (on reflection and most of the time) one most wants to gratify.

Second objection: If the thesis has now become ' "I ought to do X" amounts to saying "I most want to do X" ', it is a philosophical paradox of a familiar kind, and the general objection to all such paradoxes will apply to it.

Surely, it may be protested, we have by now learned the lesson expressed in Butler's dictum, 'Everything is what it is and not another thing.' To say that 'morality' means the same as 'what I most want' is to ignore and confuse valuable distinctions that would not have crept into ordinary speech if they had not been forced on us by the facts of moral experience. The philosopher's task is to investigate the characteristic situations in which we use this or that term, and to map the differences between them. He is doing his job best when he draws our attention to nuances that usually escape notice. He is certainly not doing it when he wilfully ignores distinctions that are perfectly obvious even to the man in the street.

The answer to this objection is that, while the differences between 'I want X' and 'I think X right' are many and important, their very existence may have prevented us from noticing resemblances that are also important, and that it is also the business of the philosopher to point out. Very well then, it may be answered, point them out. But when all the resemblances and all the differences have been noted, when both moral concepts and the concept of desire have been 'mapped', 'located in logical space', let us not throw everything into confusion again by such crass and patently false remarks as 'to say that X is right is just to say that one wants it'.

Such a remark need not, however, be confusing. To say, on *a priori* grounds, that it must be is to rule out such valuable empirical discoveries as 'a panther is just a leopard' or 'the morning star is just the evening star'. Certainly these terms would not have been distinguished in common use if there had not been some differences (indeed, quite striking ones) between panthers and leopards (their colour) and between the morning and the evening star (the time at which they are seen). These differences had, however, been thought (mistakenly) to point to further differences that did not exist. In precisely the same way, it is suggested, the differences that do exist between wanting and judging right or good have been thought (mistakenly) to point to further differences. In particular, it has been thought that the authority that attaches to moral judgements is different in origin from the authority that attaches to desire.

Third objection: Even granted that there are no good *a priori* grounds for ruling out the possibility that 'I ought to do X' amounts to saying 'X is what I most want', there is still the *a posteriori* objection that the two expressions do in fact mean very different things.

On the face of it, this seems quite true. We usually distinguish between what we want to do and what we ought to do.

Moreover, we often say such things as 'It's not that I want to do it; it's just that I think I ought'. This suggests not only that the two do not mean the same but also that very often they do not even coincide.

But consider again the shoe-buying example. Here it would be quite natural to say 'What I wanted to do was to buy the first pair of shoes I saw, and get the beastly business over, but I knew that I ought to go on looking till I found the right pair'. Yet it seems clear that the conflict is simply between two desires, the desire of the moment and the more permanent desire: the desire that was, in a sense, weaker though it proved stronger at the decisive moment and the desire that was over-riding though it was in fact over-ridden. That we use 'ought' and other moral terms in such contexts is what gives point to Samuel Butler's aphorism: 'Virtue is when the pain comes before the pleasure; vice is when the pleasure comes before the pain.' Very often, of course, the over-riding desire is what Hume called a 'calm passion'; not an urgent itch of the flesh or mind, but a strong and deeply felt desire none the less. Certainly there is nothing in these considerations that need prevent us from saying that 'what I ought to do' (get shoes that fit, in the case in question) is simply what I most want.

But, it will be objected, is not this to reduce morality to self-interest, in the crudest possible way: to identify 'I ought to do X' with 'X will give me most pleasure in the long run'? And the obvious objection to this is that we often think that we ought to do something, not because it will give us pleasure, but because it will give others pleasure. If only our own pleasure is in question, we may indeed use 'ought', but not the moral ought. 'I ought to get shoes that fit' is not a moral statement at all. On the other hand, suppose I say 'Of course what I wanted to do was to stay at home before the fire with a book, but I knew I ought to go out and visit Uncle Silas in hospital, boring old so-and-so though he is'. Here the conflict is not between my comfort at the moment and my greater comfort later on: I will always be more comfortable if I leave Uncle Silas unvisited.

Except perhaps in my conscience; but my conscience would not make me uncomfortable if my belief that I ought to visit Uncle Silas were just the belief that I would be more comfortable if I did.

It is true, I think, that 'I ought to do X' is not to be analysed as 'Doing X will give me most pleasure in the long run'. It does not follow, however, that the correct analysis is not 'Doing X is what, in the long run, I most want to do'. To explain this, it will be necessary to consider in some detail the accepted case against psychological hedonism. Briefly, that case amounts to this: that 'pleasure' (or 'liking', or 'enjoyment', or 'wanting', or whatever the key term may be in the hedonist's formulation of his position) is misleadingly ambiguous.

There is certainly a sense in which I may be said to take pleasure in someone else's pleasure, for example, Uncle Silas's, or the pleasure of the child I take to the circus. But, quite clearly, we can distinguish between his pleasure and the pleasure I take in his pleasure. So far, the psychological hedonist will probably agree. But, he will say, in trying to decide whether or not to take him to the circus, it is my pleasure in his pleasure, not his pleasure as such, that moves me. Probably the circus in itself bores me: that is to say, it causes me pain rather than pleasure. What I have to do is to weigh this pain, not against the child's pleasure, but against my pleasure in seeing him happy. If this is greater than my boredom, I will take him; but if I think that the pain of boredom will be greater than the pleasure of seeing him happy, I will not take him. The action I take will be the one from which I expect to get most pleasure on the whole. For only my pleasure can move me to action.

But, it may be objected, this is just not true. It is quite possible for me to decide that my pleasure in the child's happiness will not be greater than my boredom, and yet decide to take him. I may go to the circus reluctantly, saying to myself 'I am in for a thoroughly miserable evening'. So far as I do consider only my pleasure, including the pleasure I expect to

get out of watching the child's radiant face, I may decide that
the experience will be on the whole painful.

But, the psychological hedonist will say, you *must* want to go
more than you want to stay at home, or you would not go.
The 'must' here gives him away. Is it, we may ask, psychologically necessary or logically necessary? The psychological
hedonist puts his contention forward as a matter of psychological necessity: men are so constituted that they cannot help
choosing what gives them the greatest pleasure. This is a synthetic proposition; and it is proper to ask for the evidence on
which it is based. The evidence could only be observation of
human behaviour. One negative instance would of course refute
the assertion: one case in which a man does choose the alternative that gives him less pleasure. But, when his opponents put
forward such cases, the psychological hedonist brushes them
aside. The course chosen must give you more pleasure, he says,
or you would not choose it.

If the hedonist's claim is meant to be an empirical one, then
this is a sheer piece of dogmatism, unsupported by evidence.
But it is more likely that the psychological hedonist is changing
his ground: that he is now making an analytic statement and
not a synthetic one. It is quite safe to say that, given a free
choice, a man will choose the course he prefers; for to say that
A prefers X is just to say that he will choose X. Now it is quite
possible to use 'the course that gives A the most pleasure' to
mean 'the course that A prefers'. In that case it is true to say
that a man will always choose the course that gives him most
pleasure. True but trivial: for all that is being said is that a man
will always choose the course he chooses.

We have, then, this position: the psychological hedonist
is either making a true but trivial assertion, or making a
significant but false one. Either he is saying that the martyr
actually enjoys his martyrdom, finds it a pleasurable experience:
in which case what he is saying is false; or he is saying that, in
spite of its painfulness, the martyr prefers martyrdom to the
alternative open to him, would rather be martyred than recant,

say: in which case what he is saying is no more than we knew already. From the true assertion, moreover, none of the consequences claimed by the psychological hedonist will follow: that there is no essential difference between the martyr's motives and the sensualist's (they just happen to enjoy different things); that all men are selfish, all actions interested. These consequences follow only from the false assertion.

What makes psychological hedonism plausible is the ease with which these two assertions may be confused. The hedonist's error, then, may serve as a cautionary tale. It brings out the ambiguity of terms like 'pleasure', an ambiguity which infects nearly all the terms we might try to substitute for it. Even 'prefers', which I have used above in an attempt to avoid the ambiguity, may well be used in the same double sense.

This ambiguity has important consequences for the Butler–Hutcheson–Baier account of reasons for action. It may help us to detect further ambiguity. Consider the assertion 'That I enjoy something is a reason for doing it'. What does 'being a reason' mean? There are at least three possibilities, which need to be distinguished from each other. To say that X is a reason for me may mean: (*a*) that I find myself choosing things that are X, whether or not I know that they are; (*b*) that my knowledge that something is X leads me to choose it; (*c*) that I approve of my choosing things that are X, whether or not I do actually choose them. The distinction between (*a*) and (*b*) is the one that we usually make between a 'cause' and a 'reason'; but 'X is a reason for me' might mean either (*b*) or (*c*).

Consider the following situations:

1. Smith is fond of eating sweets. This worries him a little, as he thinks that the habit will ruin his teeth and make him fat and flabby. But one day a doctor tells him that he has a mild disorder which leads to a craving for sweets, and that he should eat as many as he wants to.

2. Jones is told by his doctor to drink milk. He hates milk, but dutifully swallows a pint every day.

Smith's disorder is the *cause* of his sweet-eating. It is not, however, his reason for eating them, at any rate before his visit to the doctor, because until then he does not know anything about it. His reason for eating them is that he finds the experience pleasurable. As a result, he chooses to eat them, in the sense that he goes on eating them, without being forced to do so by anyone else. But he does not, before his visit to the doctor, approve of his choosing to do this. After he has seen the doctor, he does approve of this choice. His disorder now is his reason (one of his reasons) for eating sweets. More accurately his reason is that he knows that he has the disorder, and that eating sweets is good for it. His belief in these propositions, plus his desire to be healthy, influence him to choose to eat sweets, much as his physical condition causes the craving which also causes him to choose to eat sweets. The two factors now co-operate. We speak of reasons as well as causes, when knowledge on Smith's part is necessary before the cause can operate. Before he sees the doctor, he does not know about the physical condition, but he does of course know that sweets taste pleasant to him.

Jones does not have this reason for drinking milk. For him, the taste of milk is a reason for not drinking it. But he has the same medical reason for drinking milk as Smith has for eating sweets. He approves of his drinking milk, and, in a sense, he wants to drink milk; he chooses to drink it, since he does in fact drink it, and nobody but himself forces it down his unwilling throat; but he does not find the experience pleasurable.

These examples bring out the differences between: (i) finding an action pleasurable, (ii) choosing to do it, (iii) approving of that choice. The psychological hedonist fails to make the distinction between enjoying an experience and choosing to have it; consequently he is led to say that self-interest is the sole human motive. If, correcting him, we say that self-interest is one reason for human actions, but not the sole reason, we may fall into a similar ambiguity. We may mean either that self-interest is a reason for doing things, or that self-interest is a reason for approving of our doing them. Jones's belief that drinking milk is good for him is not only his reason for drinking it but his reason for approving of his drinking it. Smith's belief, before his visit to the doctor, that eating sweets will be bad for him is his reason for disapproving of eating them, though it does not actually make him stop eating them.

It will be clear that what I have been mainly concerned with in this chapter is the phenomenon of approving. The man in the shoe shop, for example, did not take pleasure in continuing the search, nor did he choose to continue it. But he did approve of continuing it. The point of the example, then, is that it is possible to make these distinctions and still maintain that to approve of something is, nevertheless, to realize that one wants it more than one wants the alternatives.

Certainly it need not be my own pleasure I am thinking of, but (for example) Uncle Silas's. And we may indeed put this by saying 'I am not thinking of what I want, but of what he wants'. Or a husband may say to a wife 'I didn't want to come to this boring party in the first place; I only came because you wanted to'. It seems natural to conclude that, just as concern for one's own pleasure is not a moral motive, though concern for the pleasure of others may be, so the gratification of one's own wants is not a moral consideration, though the gratification of the wants of others may be.

Can it be said, however, that the wants of others influence us directly, and not indirectly, through wants of our own? The husband quoted above might just as easily have said 'I didn't want to come to the party, but I did want to please you'. Or the nephew of Silas may say that he wants his uncle to have the comfort of a visit. He may also decide, on reflection, that he wants to visit Uncle Silas more than he wants to stay at home, in the sense that the man in the other example wanted to get the right pair of shoes more than he wanted to be done with shopping. That this is compatible with 'Of course I didn't want to visit him at all' need not worry us. Compare 'Of course I didn't *want* to go on shopping'. Nor need it worry us that we are now involved in the paradox 'I want what Uncle

Silas wants more than I want what I want'. There is no contradiction here: only a wider and a narrower sense of 'want'.

It may, perhaps, be useful to distinguish between first-order
wants and second-order wants. 'I want (second-order) you to
get what you want (first-order).' If a husband says to his wife
'I didn't want to go to the party at all; I only went because you
wanted to', he is using 'want' to refer to first-order wants.
This distinction also enables us to make sense of 'I want
what you want more than I want what I want'. Spelled out,
this becomes 'I want (second-order) what you want (first-
order) more than I want (second-order) what I want (first-
order)'.

Two things should be noticed about this distinction. First,
it is not implied that second-order wants always over-ride first-
order wants. A father may want his child to enjoy himself by
playing a rowdy game, but may want his own peace and quiet
more. Here a first-order want over-rides a second-order want.
It might be objected that in this situation the father is saying,
in effect, 'I want what I want more than I want what he wants';
so that the conflict is, after all, between two second-order wants.
But there is something dubious about the notion that a desire
always gives rise to a further, higher-order desire that the first
desire shall be gratified. The objection is not that this would
generate an infinite series: the series is not a vicious one. It is
rather that wanting something is not, as a rule, distinguishable
from wanting that want to be gratified. The distinction arises
only when the first-order want is someone else's, not one's own,
or when the second-order want is that a first-order want of
one's own should *not* be gratified (because it conflicts with
another first-order want).

The second point to be noticed is that 'what I want for
others' is not always that their wants shall be gratified. For
instance, a mother may want her son to be a teetotaller (or a
Christian, or a stockbroker) though he does not in the least want
these things for himself. It may be objected that what the mother
really wants is to be the mother of a teetotaller (or whatever);

which is something she wants for herself, not another, though it involves another. Alternatively, she thinks that her son will be happier if he is a teetotaller (or whatever) though he does not realize this himself; in which case she does after all want his wants to be gratified, though she takes account of wants that he does not know he has, or perhaps of wants that he may come to have too late. It is not clear, however, that this is a satisfactory account of wanting someone to be happy. It is even more doubtful whether these two are the only alternatives. In general, it seems reasonable to say that one may want others to behave in a certain way (the warring factions to make peace in Vietnam, the Beatles to be given, or alternatively not to be given, M.B.E.s, homosexuals to be punished by the law) without supposing either that one is directly affected thereby, or that the people who are want these things to happen to them. The most one can be said to want for oneself is to live in a world, or perhaps a country, where matters are ordered thus and not otherwise. No doubt such desires rank among the calm passions; they may nevertheless be very strong.

But, it may be protested, is not this a *reductio ad absurdum* of your whole thesis? Would it not be simpler and more accurate to say that such attitudes are not wants at all, either for oneself or for others? They are rather rational convictions about what the world ought to be like. That it is a mistake to treat them as wants is shown by the fact that one may very well think that the world ought to be such that, for example, everyone should share in the really unpleasant work without in the least wanting such a reform to take place. Again, one may quite passionately want the prisoner in the dock to be acquitted (because one feels sorry for him) while regretfully deciding that he ought to be convicted (because he is clearly guilty). It is sheer Humean dogma to insist that such beliefs must be wants (or, more generally, 'passions') because they may move to action.

But can it be said that one really believes that such-and-such ought to be the case unless one does want it to be the case? Of course one wants other things as well, some of which may be incompatible with this one. And my contention is that, if one believes that X ought to be the case, one not merely wants X but wants it more than these other things, in the way that, in my example, the customer wants to go on trying shoes more than he wants to give up the search, even though he does in fact give up the search. It is only in the sense that one does *not* want to go on looking for shoes that one can be said not to want the more just distribution of labour, or the conviction of the guilty man. If this is not true, we are entitled to ask whether ' X ought to be the case' is a genuine belief, or merely lip-service.

Lip-service does of course complicate the matter. It has already been pointed out, more than once, that there are two uses of 'morality': one in which we may say 'Smith's morality is a purely selfish one' and one in which we may say 'Smith allows self-interest to usurp the place of morality'. Now there is no reason why Smith himself may not adopt the second usage, and say, with a sigh, 'Of course so-and-so is the moral course; I really ought to do it'. But if he has neither the least intention of doing it nor any remorse at not having done it, we can still say that his morality is indeed a purely selfish one, and that, in spite of what he says, he does not *believe* that he ought to do it.

This double sense of 'morality' does help to explain why we are reluctant to say that 'I ought' is equivalent to 'I most want': unless the desire has a certain content we are inclined to say that it cannot be a moral desire. But we are concerned here with the form, and not the content, of morality, since we are seeking a morally neutral answer to the question: what is morality? My contention is that, if a man calls X the moral course but does not in fact want it more (in the sense explained) than he wants the alternative, then he is describing, not *his* morality, but the morality of the community in general. And X would not be the moral course for the community in general unless most people did want it more than the alternative.

The answer to the third objection, then, is that, while it is true that there are important differences between 'I ought to do X' and 'X is what I most want to do', these differences are sufficiently accounted for by the following facts: (1) We are inclined to reserve 'want' for (*a*) those pressing but relatively transient desires that conflict with more settled and permanent ones, and (*b*) 'first-order' as distinct from 'second-order' wants. (2) We are inclined to reserve 'ought' and other moral terms for those wants which have a particular content: in particular, for those that are concerned with the welfare of others. This is understandable, since much social pressure is directed to ensuring that we shall subordinate our purely personal interests to those of the community in general. None of this, however, seriously affects the thesis that moral attitudes, desires, principles, etc., are distinguished from others by being over-riding.

Fourth objection: In fact, moral considerations are not always over-riding.

Morality, it may be objected, is not always over-riding, not merely in the sense that it does not always prevail, but in the sense that we do not always think that it ought to prevail. For someone might say: 'Of course the moral course here would be such-and-such (to tell the customs officer about the box of cigars you know he won't find; to go to great trouble to push your way through the crowded tram to find the conductor, who clearly won't reach you before your stop, and pay your fare; to give your real name and address to the policeman who finds you in a pub after hours, even though you know you can get away with giving a false one) but one mustn't take morality too seriously; I would do the other thing if I were you.'

The suggestion here is that moral principles draw our attention to a particular type of consideration, which is of importance, but not necessarily of supreme importance. One takes account of morality, along with all the other relevant factors, but one does not necessarily decide, or even think that one ought to decide, in favour of morality. Moral demands, it is sometimes added, are made upon us by society for its own protection: the rational man will take account of the claims of society, but will not necessarily subordinate every other kind of claim to them.

It might seem that, if it can be established that we do use 'moral' and 'morality' in this way, my contention that morality is, by definition, over-riding is completely disposed of. There is one respect, however, in which, rather oddly, this argument tends to confirm my thesis.

I have suggested that, in ordinary speech, we use 'morality' to refer to over-riding principles that have a particular content. Normally these two characteristics (being over-riding and having a certain content) go together; but sometimes they are found apart. When that happens, we sometimes use 'morality' of any over-riding principles, whatever their content ('Satan's morality', 'his morality is purely selfish') and sometimes confine the term to those over-riding principles that do have the usual content ('Satan's principles are the negation of morality', 'he allows selfishness to usurp the place of morality'). If this is accepted, it need not surprise us to find a further use of 'morality', to refer to principles with the orthodox content, even when they are not over-riding. And it is just this that the suggested examples illustrate.

One might expect this use, however, to be a somewhat marginal one. And so indeed it is. For notice the statement 'One mustn't take morality too seriously'. This clearly means 'One *ought not* to take morality too seriously'. And what kind of principle is this? Isn't it a moral principle? The suggestion is that there are two kinds of consideration jostling for attention: moral considerations and some other kind: selfish ones, perhaps. Now how does one decide between them? Perhaps by means of a further higher-order principle: 'One ought not to tell the truth, pay one's debts, etc., when the inconvenience to oneself is out of all proportion to the benefits to others', or something of that kind. But it is quite clear that this is itself a moral principle: it is indeed simply a corollary of the basic principle of utilitarian morality. In general, any principle that would enable one to say 'One ought not to follow the dictates of morality' is itself a moral principle. So that we have here two senses of 'moral': one in which it means 'over-riding', and one (almost an 'inverted commas use') in which it means 'the over-riding principles most people subscribe to'. Almost an inverted commas use, because there would not seem to be much difference between saying 'One ought not to follow the dictates of morality' and 'The dictates in question are not really moral'.

But, it may be said, this is to miss the whole point of the objection; and, moreover, to distort it. Of course one cannot say, without contradiction, 'One ought not to do what morality dictates', for that is to say 'One ought not to do what one ought to do'. But a man may very well say 'Of course that is what you ought to do; but don't do it'. It is not that he does not subscribe to the moral rule: he does. It is not that he is proposing an alternative moral rule. He is simply in favour of breaking the moral rule we already have.

But what does 'in favour of' mean here? There would seem to be two possibilities. It may be that, without dissenting from the rule, one breaks it without much compunction because it is a minor one, or because, even though the general principle may be important, the breach in these circumstances is a minor one. Or it may be that one does genuinely approve of breaking the rule in all circumstances, advises others to break it, and so on. In that case, it is hard to see in what sense one can be said to subscribe to the rule. In what sense, indeed, does one regard it as a moral rule at all? If a man tells us that he accepts such-and-such a set of moral principles, and then not only violates them without compunction but consistently advises us to violate them too, we will certainly be inclined to say that his real morality is not what he says it is.

My point, however, is not that a particular definition of morality tells us what it 'really' is. All the senses of morality that have been distinguished are perfectly legitimate ones. My point is simply that none of them need throw doubt on the contention that men do in fact form a fairly coherent set of principles (or attitudes, since they need not be formulated explicitly) in accordance with which they settle conflicts between their various desires; that when they do not act in accordance with these principles or attitudes they feel a peculiar uneasiness; and that, in one perfectly intelligible sense of the term, these principles or attitudes constitute a man's morality, whatever their content.

Fifth objection: 'I ought to do X' does not always imply that X is to be preferred to any alternative.

There is a different way in which moral principles may be said not to be over-riding. Suppose someone is faced with a difficult choice between two duties: between helping his aged and poverty-stricken parents, let us say, and providing for his own children, when he has not enough money to do both. Eventually he makes his decision, let us say in favour of his children. He has no doubt that it is the right one: but his other obligation has not thereby been extinguished. In a sense, he still ought to help his parents, even though this duty is in fact over-ridden by another one.[1]

I have said 'in a sense', because there are some who will deny that in these circumstances he ought to help his parents. The disagreement is, however, rather about the use of the word 'ought' here than about anything else. It is common ground that the man has not done anything wrong and is in no way to be blamed for not fulfilling his obligation to his parents. Williams's point is that a conflict of duties is significantly different from a conflict of beliefs:

...in the belief case, my concern to get things straight is a concern both to find the right belief (whichever it may be) and to be disembarrassed of the false belief (whichever it may be), whereas in the moral case my concern is not in the same way to find the right item and be rid of the other...I do not think in terms of banishing error. I think, if constructively at all, in terms of acting for the best, and this is a frame of mind that *acknowledges* the presence of both the two 'oughts'.[2]

'X is over-ridden by Y', then, is, on this view, consistent with the truth of 'I ought to do X'; which might seem to be

[1] See B. A. O. Williams, 'Ethical Consistency', in Aristotelian Society, *Supplementary Proceedings*, XXXIX (1965), 103–24.
[2] *Ibid.* p. 110.

fatal to my thesis. Actually, however, I think it can be shown that this view is not only consistent with, but lends some support to, that thesis. Briefly, I shall argue that there are here two senses of 'ought', neither of which can be dispensed with; and that there are two, at least partly parallel, senses of 'over-riding'.

In one sense, if it is agreed that my duty to do X is out-weighed by my duty to do Y, then it follows that, in this situation, X is not what I ought to do: on the contrary, what I ought to do is Y. In another sense, however, X is still something I ought to do: in general, if not in this situation; and even in this situation, in that the obligation remains, even though I cannot fulfil it.

'Over-riding' is a relative term. In the shoe example, my desire for foot comfort over-rides my desire to avoid the trouble of shopping. But there are many other considerations that this one would not over-ride: it does not, actually, stand very high in the moral peck-order. This may explain why we are reluctant to call it a moral consideration. In the particular situation, it over-rides the conflicting consideration: this is, as we have seen, enough to induce us to say 'I ought to have gone on looking' and to feel guilt. In general, however, it is not the kind of consideration that over-rides most others: not, in that sense, an over-riding consideration. That one's parents need help is, however, precisely this kind of consideration. The desire for foot comfort, then, though over-riding in the par-ticular case, is not in general an over-riding consideration. In one sense gratifying it is something I ought to do, but not in another. The desire to help one's parents, on the other hand, though over-ridden in the particular case, is in general an over-riding consideration. In one sense gratifying it is something we ought to do, but not in another.

The general point is that a morality is a fairly settled policy of preferring one kind of consideration, end, attitude, etc., to another kind. Hence conflicts within that kind strike us as con-flicts within morality; conflicts between a consideration of that kind and one of another kind as conflicts between morality and something else; conflicts between two considerations of another kind as conflicts wholly outside morality. Yet the shoe- buying example would suggest that even the first and the third of these resemble each other quite closely: closely enough to enable us to say that, in all three, the question at issue is, after all, about what I most want.

CHAPTER 18

EPILOGUE

In this book I have been arguing for a subjectivist and naturalist position in ethics. Such a position is likely to be misunderstood. To many it seems merely nihilist, and incompatible with any moral convictions. To others it seems at least to deny reason and argument any place in morality. It may be as well, therefore, without recapitulating the arguments I have used, to state very briefly the main contentions which I have been defending. These are:

(1) Men form relatively settled policies (which need not be consciously formulated) of deciding between alternative courses of conduct by preferring one type of consideration to another, and so allowing one type of desire to over-ride another type of desire. Such a policy may be quite complex, in that desires of type A may over-ride desires of type B in one set of circumstances, and that desires of type B may over-ride desires of type A in different circumstances: it is no part of my thesis that every man arranges his desires in a simple hierarchy. Moreover, most men do, perhaps quite frequently, gratify desires that are not over-riding even when they conflict with ones that are: in which case they feel guilt.

(2) Such a policy constitutes a man's morality. Consequently A's morality may differ from B's. There are, however, psychological and sociological factors that cause men's moralities to resemble one another quite closely, especially within the same culture.

(3) If A's morality does differ from B's, each will think the other wrong. It does not follow that neither is really right or wrong; for to say that is to assume the very objectivist view of morality that is here being contested. What does follow is that neither can be accused of making an error about a matter of fact. But this does not mean that there is nothing to choose

between the two moralities. One may (for example) reveal callousness and narrowness of sympathy; the other kindness and sensitiveness to the feelings of others. Whether you think this good or bad will depend on your own moral attitudes; but, if you do, as a result of your own approval of sympathy and sensitiveness, condemn a callous morality, you will really condemn it: genuinely think it bad, oppose it, dispraise it and strive against it.

If, on the other hand, you adopt a different morality, you will not of course think of it as callous and insensitive, but as manly and realistic; and you will think of the policy you reject as sentimental and squeamish. In this case, too, you will genuinely condemn such a policy and regard it as genuinely wrong.

(4) It does not follow, either, that reason and argument are out of place in moral matters. Both are in place: (*a*) because most moral disagreement is not about fundamental moral assumptions, but either about relevant matters of fact or about secondary conclusions thought (sometimes mistakenly) to follow from the basic assumptions; (*b*) because, for psychological and social reasons, men do agree pretty well in their basic moral assumptions; (*c*) because it is not always easy to determine what one's own basic moral assumptions are. To say that moral beliefs, or attitudes, are ultimately subjective is not to say that they are arbitrary, or that we can assume them at will. We have the moral attitudes we have because we are the sort of men we are. Much moral argument consists in reviewing various kinds of real or imaginary situation so that we may discover what kinds of situation we really approve, and what features of them make us approve them. To discover this is to discover, not objective truths about the world, but what our own moral attitudes are, and so what manner of men we are.

To adopt a moral policy is not merely to decide, in a moment of enthusiasm, that henceforth we will be (let us say) careless adventurers, using other people as mere tools for our own advancement or pleasure; or (in a different mood) dedicated ascetics scorning fleshly delights and interested only in the contemplative and spiritual life; or (under another influence) solid and sensible citizens, determined not to be too different from the man next door. To adopt any such policy is to accept all the consequences of following it; and we may find that we do not like the consequences: not merely that we do not enjoy the resulting way of life, and the responses that such conduct evokes in other people, but that we do not, once we fully understand the implications, really admire the sort of persons we are trying to become. Moral reasoning and argument consists in exploring such implications.

(5) Hare is, I think, right in saying that one useful way to explore the implications of a policy is to ask ourselves whether we would be prepared to accept the role of any of the persons affected by such a policy. One reason for this is that other people are likely to feel justified in treating us as we treat them, so that the actual consequence of adopting a particular policy is, as a rule, to be on the receiving end of it. This is not a logical point, but a practical one; and there are, of course, situations in which it would not apply.

There is, however, another reason. There is, I have argued, nothing irrational about treating other people differently from oneself simply on the ground that we are we and they are they. To say, as Hare does, that such conduct is (by definition) not moral is not to give a reason for abstaining from it. (To say that it does give one is to rely on a different definition of 'moral'.) But, as we have seen, the rational egoist will try to induce others to act in a way which he does not admire. There is nothing irrational about this: however reprehensible it may be, it is not irrational for a salesman (for example) to try to induce a customer to buy something for a price he would not pay himself. The salesman will not, however, admire the dupe; whereas he will, if he approves of his own conduct, admire another shrewd salesman. This does not mean that 'admire' and 'approve' have the principle of universalizability built into them. The salesman does not issue the imperative: 'Let me be swindled if ever I encounter a shrewder salesman than myself.' He does not in the least want this to come about; he does not, in Hare's sense, 'accept' this consequence.

It is, then, logically possible to admire and approve of conduct (in our example, the saleman's wiles) which, if applied to oneself, one would dislike and resist. But, though logically possible, it is not psychologically possible for most of us. For it involves trying to induce others to act in a way (in this case, the way in which a simple customer acts) which, in our secret hearts, we regard as irrational. If this is not to involve self-deception (in which case it would be irrational) it must certainly involve the deception of others; and a deliberate policy of deception and hypocrisy is abhorrent to most of us. To treat others as one would wish to be treated oneself is, I have argued, not a logical principle; I do not deny that it is a quite fundamental moral principle which nearly all men do in fact accept.

(6) This book has been concerned with the ontological status of moral principles. I have argued that they are expressions of over-riding desires. To say this is not in the least to diminish their force or their importance.

INDEX

Index